SEVEN MASTERS, ONE PATH

SEVEN MASTERS, ONE PATH

Meditation Secrets from the World's Greatest Teachers

John Selby

HarperSanFrancisco

A Division of HarperCollins*Publishers*

SEVEN MASTERS, ONE PATH: MEDITATION SECRETS FROM THE WORLD'S GREATEST TEACHERS. Copyright © 2003 by John Selby. All rights reserved. Printed in the United States of America. No part of this book may be used or reproduced in any manner whatsoever without written permission except in the case of brief quotations embodied in critical articles and reviews. For information address HarperCollins Publishers, Inc., 10 East 53rd Street, New York, NY 10022.

HarperCollins books may be purchased for educational, business, or sales promotional use. For information please write: Special Markets Department, HarperCollins Publishers, Inc., 10 East 53rd Street, New York, NY 10022.

HarperCollins Web site: http://www.harpercollins.com
HarperCollins®, ♛®, and HarperSanFrancisco™ are trademarks of HarperCollins Publishers, Inc.

FIRST EDITION

Text Design by Martha Blegen

Library of Congress Cataloging-in-Publication Data is available upon request.
ISBN 0–06–052251–8 (cloth)

06 07 ❖ RRD(H) 10 9 8 7 6 5 4

Contents

Acknowledgments

I would like to offer humble thanks to the following contemporary teachers who personally took considerable time to point me toward a deeper understanding of the meditative process, and also offered specific spiritual insights that are now shared in this book: Alan Watts, Krishnamurti, Richard Alpert, Rebecca Oriard, Bill Gearhart, Rollo May, Humphrey Osmond, Thakin Kung, Carl Rogers, Birgitta Steiner, Kriyananda, and Samuel Lewis. There are of course many recognized and unrecognized teachers along the meditative path, and I'm thankful to everyone who has contributed to the deeper understanding of how our minds work and how meditation is best experienced.

SEVEN MASTERS,
ONE PATH

Succeeding with Meditation

Look within—and be still
Free from fear and attachment
Know the sweet joy of the way . . .
Buddha

The Ojai Valley, nestled quietly at the foot of the Topa Topa Mountains about thirty miles inland from Santa Barbara, is said to have been the spiritual heartland of the ancient Chumash civilization that once thrived along the California coast. As fate would have it, the Spanish invasion in the 1600s wiped out the Chumash, and for a couple hundred years the Ojai Valley was mostly unoccupied except for a few faltering Spanish land-grant families and the usual proliferation of native wildlife.

In 1906, at the age of seventeen, my grandfather (also named John Selby) moved from his birthplace nearby in Ventura into the solitary Ojai Valley and became one of the first cattle ranchers of the area. Over the ensuing years the unique combination of lingering Native American spiritual energies, my grandfather's natural mystic propensities, and the earthly intensity of such a remarkably beautiful natural setting somehow evoked a special quality of consciousness in Gramps. As more settlers moved in during the first part of the new century, he became recognized throughout the region as a rancher packing a special spiritual charge. During the 1940s and 1950s more and more people came to know and love him as the valley's indigenous spiritual master. In the 1960s CBS television even sent a film crew up to the ranch to shoot a half-hour network special on the silent sage of the valley.

Gramps, of course, just laughed at such attention and went on about his quiet way, teaching almost entirely through example rather than words. I had the good fortune to live with my family on my grandfather's ranch throughout much of my childhood and spent most of my free time helping him with his daily chores and ranch projects—walking behind him quietly along game trails, learning to laugh rather than curse when upsetting difficulties arose, riding our horses through oak woods and open meadows, sitting half an hour at a time without speaking beside swift-running streams . . . and discovering by osmosis how this man purposefully kept his thinking mind mostly quiet as he observed the world without judgment, treated every one of God's creatures with respect and compassion, and held his focus on being loving and receptive rather than slipping into all the various human fears and ego-games.

Later I would study with a number of the world's recognized masters and learn their formal meditation techniques. However, in all honesty, most of the meditative understandings I'll be sharing with you in this book were ones I first experienced early in life and quite beyond any organized format, through this simple man's depthless spiritual example. Gramps truly lived in Spirit and showed me that the spiritual path is to be found beyond all dogmas and separatist religious belief systems.

Perhaps most important for this book, the meditative lesson that Gramps imprinted on my soul was that meditation is not something to be done once or twice a day—it's a full-time spiritual ambiance that ideally permeates every moment of our lives. Gramps regularly would pause when things got too hectic, lean against a fence post or sit down for just a few minutes, and allow his usual radiant demeanor to return to him. Such short meditative breaks seemed an integral part of his daily life.

Gramps also had a formal meditation routine of sorts, in that he almost always got up at dawn and was out sitting under his favorite oak tree, weather permitting, when the sun rose. I would often get up in time to sit with him quietly as the sun came up, enjoying the special state of mind that came to me when we were quiet together for fifteen or twenty minutes. He also regularly paused at sunset to sit down, relax . . and simply "be" as the sun disappeared. He didn't "go off" anywhere during his sun meditations; in fact, one of his strongest characteristics was an intense and continual involvement with the present moment.

Pause and Reflect

You might want to pause a moment here to reflect upon any childhood influences who deeply moved you spiritually as you were growing up. Who were they? What did you learn from them? Are they still with you in spirit?

Cognitive Liberation

A few decades after Gramps moved into the Ojai Valley, a number of spiritual communities migrated to this peaceful region to establish their various schools and teachings. One of these was the Theosophical Society, which shortly after the turn of the last century searched through India and identified a young boy there as the next world messiah, the living incarnation of Jesus and Lord

Krishna. The Theosophists took Jiddhu Krishnamurti to Europe and then in 1921 brought him on over to Ojai to mature spiritually and physically into manhood.

While living a few miles up into the orange groves from Ojai, Krishnamurti had his first "awakening" experience—and soon thereafter shocked the thousands of his devout followers by rejecting his identity as the new messiah. I myself was touched to the core when, as a young boy, I first heard him speaking in the oak groves of Ojai. I could sense that here was someone expressing in words what my grandfather expressed through his actions—that to attain peace of mind and clarity of vision, we must learn to master our own minds and tune in to our inner center beyond our cultural conditioning and religious beliefs.

Since that first encounter with Krishnamurti, I had many informal chats with him and attended formal gatherings with him; right up to our last meeting in Switzerland just before his death, I found his cut-to-the-bone teachings the clearest of any spiritual teacher in the world. In many ways, this book is my new expression, in a format the present generation can readily access, of the meditative wisdom and cognitive liberation that Krishnamurti taught to all those who had ears to hear. These insights ring with the veracity of the ancient masters and the immediate example of my own grandfather, in a new conceptual format to inspire our emerging world society.

Living Teachers

One of Krishnamurti's primary teachings was that we do best on the spiritual path, not by becoming a worshipful devotee of any particular guru, but rather by seeking our own inner center and thus tapping the perennial wisdom directly. However, he did encourage me as a young man to get out into the world and ex-

plore firsthand the techniques and teachings of the world's vast meditative tradition—in order to see clearly the need for genuine revolution in our society. When out in the world, he said, "It becomes obvious that there must be a total revolution. A different kind of culture must come into being. Unless there is deep psychological revolution, mere reformation on the periphery will have little effect. And this psychological revolution—which I think is the only revolution—is possible through meditation."

With such encouragement, I began at the age of nineteen to seek out and study with a number of prominent teachers, each of whom held a particular key to the secrets of successful meditation, rooted in the teachings of the ancient masters and also in their own insights and inspirations. This book is a direct outcome of that lifelong exploration.

At the same time, I became very curious about the scientific aspects of the meditative experience and spent many years studying the formal psychological and neurological understandings of the spiritual experience. In this realm of inquiry, one of my teachers, the admittedly flawed but brilliant Zen scholar Alan Watts challenged me to continue working on a key project he had initiated identifying the fundamental psychological principle and procedure common to all the world's great meditative traditions, and the teaching this procedure to the world.

Accepting this challenge, I soon found myself engaged in research for the National Institute of Mental Health (NIMH participated in seminal meditation studies in the 1960s and that helped shed light on our scientific comprehension of the tative experience. After many years of research in this dir slowly became clear to me that, indeed, all of the wor meditation techniques are grounded in a unified psycho derstanding of how the mind works and how we can expand consciousness toward the deeper realms of spi ness. This book offers the essential realizations of

showing how the seven great masters of the world spiritual community were all teaching key aspects or phases of the same underlying meditative process.

What Is New in This Approach?

Almost all world cultures have developed deep meditation traditions, some dating back to prehistory. There's surely nothing new under the sun in terms of the basic natural process through which the human mind opens up to, contemplates, and merges with the divine.

No matter what our theological or philosophical beliefs, the actual direct spiritual experience that lies beyond human ideas and thoughts is universal. For this reason, this meditation program works equally well if you are a Christian or a Taoist, a Hindu or a Buddhist, a Theosophist or scientist—or whatever.

This meditation program revolutionizes our capacity for success in learning to meditate by stripping away all the religious dogma and ritual and theology surrounding the human meditative experience, so as to expose the underlying psychological process taught throughout the ages by the world's great meditation teachers.

Through researching this common psychological process that underlies all the great meditative traditions, my colleagues and I have been able to develop a new meditation program that integrates all the various traditional approaches into a unified experiential whole.

There are five key innovations that make the *Seven Masters, One Path* meditation program unique and important to seeking deeper meditative experience and realization:

INNOVATION 1: THE SEVEN EXPANSIONS

ost spiritual teachers agree that meditation is best defined as the
:thodical expansion of human consciousness beyond acquired be-

liefs and attitudes about life so as to encounter a deeper reality directly. We found in our studies that there are seven primary expansions of consciousness that occur naturally during any successful meditation session. The human mind clearly advances toward spiritual bliss and realization through a predictable process when unobstructed by mental habits, disturbing emotions, or restricting beliefs. A clear presentation of this seven-step expansion process lies at the heart of the *Seven Masters, One Path* meditation program.

INNOVATION 2: QUIET-MIND TECHNIQUE

Learning to quiet our busy and often disruptive thoughts during meditation has always been a primary challenge. While doing mind research with NIMH, my colleagues and I identified a special perceptual process that instantly and predictably quiets the flow of thoughts through the mind. By learning this simple method for quieting the mind, you can advance into deep meditation.

INNOVATION 3: SHORT-FORM APPROACH

Meditation is usually seen as requiring at least half an hour of dedicated time in order to be effective. However, we've found that this assumption is not psychologically valid. By applying new insights into the meditative process, we've developed a "short-form" approach to meditation that you can move through in a remarkably short but effective time frame. Once you get good at the mental expansion process, you'll be able to move through a full meditation within whatever time period you have available, thus integrating meditation fully into every part of your busy life.

INNOVATION 4: FOCUS PHRASES

Another innovation we're introducing here that will make it easier, more effective, and more enjoyable to learn meditation is the employment of seven very carefully developed "focus phrases" that turn your mind's inner attention directly toward each of the seven expansions. Once you've moved through the initial training program, these special sayings will immediately stimulate the entire experience associated with each expansion.

INNOVATION 5: ONLINE AUDIO-GUIDANCE

The final innovation that makes the *Seven Masters, One Path* meditation practice truly effective for everyone desiring deeper contact with their inner core of being is our online dimension to the training program, available to you for free at www.7masters.com. Traditionally, students have learned to meditate by listening to the voice of their teacher guiding them through the process over and over until they internalize the process. Such direct guidance is not possible through written media. However, you can now go online and immediately access each of the seven meditative expansions.

The Learning Process

This book is very much a learning manual rather than just a philosophical discussion. My primary intent is to make sure you master each meditative expansion. Toward this aim, each chapter concludes with a guided meditation based on the actual verbal guidance I use with students and clients in person.

My intent throughout is to provide you with just enough insight and guidance to bring you to the point where your own inner meditation experience takes off and flies on its own . . . as you regularly tune in to your breathing, quiet your thoughts, focus on each of the seven meditative themes, and become fully engaged in the uniqueness of your own, always new meditative moment.

In this spirit, each chapter introduces you to a teacher, a meditation process, and a new inner experience—until you've learned by heart the seven short yet potent meditative expansions that, taken together, constitute a beautiful, powerful, and complete meditation program. In each chapter, I'll also offer short meditative pauses—places in your reading where you can put the book aside and reflect on or experience what you've just read, so that throughout the book your actual experience remains dominant over intellectual cogitation.

Those of you who are new to meditation will want to take plenty of time to explore each expansion before moving on to the next one. There's no hurry, no rush, no ultimate goal or achievement. What's important is your dedicated attention to the full experience of each new emerging meditative moment.

Others of you may have already heard about the general meditative experience, read some books on the topic, perhaps tried one or more traditional techniques, but never found a spiritual practice that you could really call your own. With this background, you'll be able to move perhaps more rapidly through the learning process—but still be sure to take your time to fully understand and experience the expansions, one at a time.

Still others of you may have already advanced quite far on your meditative journey, yet seek a more integrated and effective daily practice to enlighten your lives. Please feel free to move rapidly through discussions in this book that cover ground you may already know . . . and at the same time, do be sure to pause and experience each expansion in the formats presented here.

By moving through the insights and experiences that emerge spontaneously as you progress through this seven-expansion meditation program, you'll discover a lifetime of spiritual exploration and awakening. Feel entirely free to move at your own pace. Soon you will be able to move effortlessly through the full meditation process on your own, with no need for external guidance.

Short-Form Meditation

Traditionally you would meditate, especially in the Hindu and Buddhist format, once or twice a day for at least half an hour at a time. This framework is still highly recommended if you can manage in your busy life to set aside this length of time each day at a regular hour.

However many people today find that they might have five short meditation opportunities each day, rather than time for one long meditation period. Also, some people like to hold still for a long time, while people with different temperaments may prefer to be more on the go. And there are people like me who enjoy a regular morning or evening meditation for thirty minutes to an hour, but also benefit greatly from pausing for just five to ten minutes a number of times during the day to move through a shorter meditation that rapidly brings our consciousness into a more peaceful, insightful, and loving mode.

Having long ago found "short-form" meditation experiences to be of great value, I've explored in recent research the most effective way to tap meditation's rejuvenating powers rapidly. The seven-step meditation program you have in hand is formally called a "modular meditation" process—modular because each of the meditations stands on its own as a short yet complete meditation. At the same time, when put together in proper order, the seven meditations also work as a whole as you flow from theme to theme, being taken deeper and deeper with each modular addition.

We'll explore in more depth how you can develop your own ideal structure for meditation, one that allows you to focus on whatever meditative theme is most important for you each new day. The aim is to make sure that wherever you are, and no matter how little time you might have, you can always turn your mind toward your inner spiritual center and receive the multitudinous benefits of the meditative experience.

At the heart of this unique and perhaps radical approach to meditation is the lesson I learned early on from my grandfather, and then from Krishnamurti as well—that our spiritual aim is not to retreat once or twice a day for meditation, but to learn how to live every moment of our lives in touch with our spiritual core.

New Guidance Formats

Meditation, being the most powerful mind tool ever developed, has traditionally been passed on directly from one person to another, not through written formats but through word of mouth. We tend to learn best when listening to a voice guiding us through a process, rather than just reading about it. The spoken voice of a teacher has vastly greater impact on stimulating inner experience than do the same words when read on the page.

To learn a meditative process, you need to move through the same basic inner focusing activity in your mind a number of times . . . until you internalize the meditation process as a beautiful mental habit that you can move through without guidance. Most people resist reading the same instructions over and over so as to memorize a process, but they're quite happy to close their eyes, make no mental effort, and listen to a voice guiding them again and again through the meditative process until they "get it" and no longer need the spoken guidance.

With this reality in mind, over the last decade my colleagues and I have been busy developing a new system for delivering spoken meditative guidance at a distance—thanks to the instant streamed-audio capabilities of the Internet and also audio CD formats. Our intent has been to expand the concept of "learning from a distance" to include audio-guidance.

Thus, you'll find at the end of each chapter of this book an Internet address that you can go to at www.7masters.com that will allow you instant free access to the spoken guidance that makes learning these meditations more effortless and effective. You'll find both short meditations for when you have just a few minutes to pause and turn inward, and longer variations on the basic seven-expansion process for when you have longer periods of ten, twenty, or thirty minutes to devote to meditation.

Of course, many of you will find the written directions more than adequate and will master the meditations without audio support. But for those who want more help, just turn to your computer, get online at our website, and I'll be there. You'll also have the opportunity at www.7masters.com to join chat rooms and share your new meditation experience with other people who are reading this book. A great deal of background information on each of the seven masters, and much more, is also available online. And for those of you who don't have a computer, the seven meditations are also available in an inexpensive CD format (see back of book).

The Seven Masters

You might be wondering how I chose, from all the spiritual teachers of all time, the seven masters featured in this book. Clearly the first five masters—Patanjali, Lao Tzu, Buddha, Jesus, and Mohammed—were remarkable world teachers who not only touched my own soul with their teachings, insights, and techniques but stand eternally at the center of the world's largest spiritual movements.

The last two I chose, Gurdjieff and Krishnamurti, perfectly round off our meditation process because, along with their special impact on my own understanding of meditation, they have made new contributions and provided examples to provoke the world community's ongoing spiritual advancement.

As we'll discover here, all true spiritual teachers lead their students toward the same ultimate realization and experience—that of full immersion in the spiritual core of being that we all share, and from which we all draw our deeper sustenance, wisdom, vitality, and insight.

Let me now introduce these seven masters, who, through the ages or more recently, have powerfully awakened special spiritual realms of consciousness in a great many hearts throughout the world, and who continue to touch us directly through meditation. At the same time I'll introduce the seven "focus phrases" that you'll be learning and using during your meditations. These focus phrases will be all you need to remember, after your training period, to move fully through the entire meditation process.

PATANJALI

Nearly four thousand years ago in India, the formal study of meditation was initiated by ancient yogic masters who advanced, step by step through inward inquiry and exploration, toward a concise understanding of how our minds work and how we can employ meditation to awaken our deeper spiritual consciousness. After two thousand years of such development, a remarkable sage named Patanjali (Pah-TAN-jah-lee) brought all these teachings and insights together, and wrote detailed instructions on the art of meditation and devotion in his "Yoga Sutras."

Central to Patanjali's teaching was the idea that dedicated awareness of one's own breathing is central to all meditation, and that particular breathing techniques can alter consciousness in quite specific spiritual directions. The Sanskrit term *prana*, meaning "breath" or "life-force," has been a central concept throughout Hindu devotional history. In fact, as we'll see, almost all meditation traditions focus on a deep inner exploration of the experience of breathing.

Drawing from Patanjali's seminal teachings on *pranayama* (breath awareness and control) meditation, we'll learn the essential beginning meditation for turning the mind's full attention to the breath experience.

- The verbal expression of the first expansion of our seven-step meditation will be: "I am breathing freely."

LAO TZU

Also coming into being almost four thousand years ago, over the mountains in China, was the Taoist meditative tradition, which step by step developed primal insights regarding how to contact the divine directly through inner experience. At the very center of the Chinese tradition of spiritual realization we find the ancient Taoist teacher Lao Tzu, author of one of the most widely read spiritual texts of humankind, the *Tao Te Ching*.

When I first began studying with Alan Watts, he happened to be completing his own translation of the original Mandarin text of the *Tao Te Ching*. While observing Alan's pleasurable struggles with his translation work and attending his seminars on the Taoist text, I came to understand that the ultimate goal of the Taoist meditator is to simply quiet the flow of thoughts through the mind so as to become conscious of the deeper "whole" nature of life.

Drawing from Lao Tzu's words and suggestions, and from the general Taoist and Zen approach to meditation, we'll learn a very practical technique (a merger of ancient Taoist breath meditation with new scientific insights) for quieting the flow of thoughts through the mind at will, so as to discover experientially the core of meditation's power and beauty.

- The verbal expression of the second step in our seven-step meditation will be: "My mind is now quiet."

BUDDHA

Siddhartha Gautama was born about a hundred years after Lao Tzu, and four hundred years before Jesus, into a wealthy Hindu family in India. He experienced his total awakening when he was twenty-nine. His primary teachings show that we are all caught up in judgmental and fearful thoughts and attitudes that generate chronic suffering, and that only through looking directly at these mental habits and taking control over how we use our minds, can we break free from generating more suffering.

His key meditative teaching was that as long as we refuse to accept the reality of the present moment unequivocally, we create ongoing inner trauma—and thus keep ourselves separate from our true Buddha nature. Our chronic judgments and refusals to accept the world just as it is turn life into a living hell. By managing our minds and actions in more reality-based ways, we can transform our moment-to-moment experience from suffering into joy.

The third meditation step we'll be learning in this book focuses on learning to accept life just as it is, rather than judging the world or ourselves as somehow wrong, bad, incomplete, or just not good enough. Through total acceptance of the truth of who we really are, we can approach and even attain liberation from suffering.

- The verbal expression of the third step in our seven-step meditation will be: "I accept the world just as it is."

JESUS

The teachings of Jesus can be seen from many different perspectives and have been interpreted theologically by literally hundreds of quite varying sects and movements. For our meditative purposes here, we don't have to assume any particular theological dogma in order to understand the fundamentals of awakening that Jesus taught. In regard to the meditative path, Jesus essentially agreed entirely with Buddha, Lao Tzu, and Patanjali—that being in touch with the inner "breath of God" is an essential aspect of the spiritual path; that peace of mind and inner quiet are essential practices to nurture; that we must stop judging and accept God's creation just as it is; and most important perhaps . . . that love is the epicenter of all spiritual life.

The fourth expansion of our meditation path focuses on Jesus' powerful teachings about love and the centrality of the heart in spiritual practice. We'll draw from his own words on the theme of unconditional love and learn to put those words into practice as we discover how focusing directly on our own heart center enables us to become more radiant with love in all our relationships.

- The verbal expression of the fourth step in our seven-step meditation will be: "I love myself just as I am."

MOHAMMED

Meditatively speaking, the great gift that Mohammed brought to his Islamic culture, beginning in the sixth century A.D., was the surety that there is only one infinite spiritual power, that this power is ultimately loving and forgiving, and that this power sees human beings as basically good and harmonious. A primary root of the word *Islam* is "peace." This peace is attained in meditation by surrendering one's whole being to Allah, allowing God's love to heal all of life's various conflicts and disappointments and confusions of the mind and emotions, so that the person, the family, and the community "dwell in God" and flourish in peace.

The meditative expansion we now draw on for our fifth meditation is this process of fully surrendering to God (by whatever name) and opening our hearts to receive God's healing touch, guidance, and infinite love into our daily lives. Such surrendering and "opening up to receive" take us right to the core of spiritual awakening. Through this full surrender to God's will and help, our negative feelings of fear and anxiety are relaxed, and related hostilities and judgments are dissolved in turn. The result is an experience of deep emotional healing and peace.

- The verbal expression of the fifth expansion will be: "My heart is open to receive God's healing help."

GURDJIEFF

Emerging in the eighth and ninth centuries from Jewish, Christian, and Muslim realms of the Middle East, as well as from other mystic traditions, the Sufi spiritual movement spread throughout central Asia and eastern Europe and down into Africa. A most powerful teacher to emerge from this expansive, joy-focused tradition was George Ivanovitch Gurdjieff, a Greek-Armenian mystic and teacher of sacred dances and meditations whose significance and impact on the world's spiritual community is still just beginning to be recognized and integrated.

One of the primary techniques to emerge from Gurdjieff's teaching, usually referred to as "self-remembering," fits perfectly into our meditation program. This deep awareness technique enables us to be more conscious and more fully alive in the present moment. It builds on what we've already learned in the five previous meditations and expands our meditation to include not only our inner experience but also our interactions with the world around us.

- The verbal expression of the sixth expansion will be: "I know who I am."

KRISHNAMURTI

Krishnamurti takes us into the final expansion in our daily meditative journey, where, with our minds quiet and fully attentive to the present moment, we once again allow thoughts to flow through our minds—while we maintain a clear sense of being an observer watching our thoughts, rather than identifying with our thoughts. In such a state of expanded consciousness, we find that our thoughts are often of a mystical or insightful nature and inspired, leading to sudden realizations that can transform our lives.

In the middle of such inspirations, we often enter into a state where words fall away and we're immersed in the bliss of pure existence in the present moment. Having now explored the full expansion of our meditation process, we are free to enter into a pure state of oneness with the divine . . . and to do so each time we meditate, whether for five minutes or two hours . . . and as we complete the seventh expansion, we find that we once again are at the beginning, simply being aware of our breathing . . . in bliss.

• The verbal expression of the seventh expansion will be: "I am here, now, in bliss."

The Seven Meditations

I'd like to introduce you quickly to each of the meditations that you'll be mastering in this program, so that you have in your mind the full flow of experiences that make up the complete meditation process. You'll see that there's a natural progression from the first meditation to the second, from the second to the third, and so forth to the seventh. There is in fact an extremely tight psychological as well as spiritual logic for the order and progression of these meditations.

BREATH AWARENESS

Almost all meditative traditions begin (and sometimes end, as in Zen) with the primal experience of focusing our mind's attention directly toward the present-moment happening of our own breathing. The physiological process of breathing is without question our most vital and immediate life activity. We possess the power to control our breathing at will, and also to set our breathing totally free, as we become fully conscious of the infinite depths of consciousness that spring into being when we hold our breathing as a primary spiritual focus.

QUIETING THE MIND

Many people confuse praying, in which we're "talking to God," with meditation, in which our talking, thinking minds become quiet and we enter the universe of consciousness that exists only when the flow of thoughts through our minds temporarily stops. Likewise, meditation is often confused with contemplation, in which we reflect (often with very active cognitive minds) on the theme of the contemplation. Quieting our minds involves distancing ourselves from, and then gently quieting altogether, the flow of thoughts through the mind. This is the second essential step in a complete meditative practice—and luckily recent mind research has shown us new ways to achieve this ancient goal.

ACCEPTING THE TRUTH

One of the great abilities of the human mind—and equally one of its main curses—is its unrelenting capacity to judge what's happening to ourselves and the world around us. We inherit and create beliefs about how we think the world should be, and then we reject anything that doesn't fit into our belief system. Meditation requires temporarily putting aside that judgmental activity of the mind so that we can see the truth clearly, accept reality as it is, and thus set ourselves free from the blinding effect of chronic judging and all its resultant heartaches.

HEART AWAKENING

Directly in the middle of our seven meditative practices is the remarkable quality of love—the ability of the heart to awaken to deeper spiritual levels of compassion. Meditation without a central focus on love is no meditation at all. Each and every spiritual tradition of the world holds love as crucial, and direct awareness of one's heart center as primary. The universal equation "God is

Love" stands as the foundation of meditation. Our challenge is to master a simple yet profound meditation that amplifies our own capacity to both receive and spread love in the world.

EMOTIONAL HEALING

Psychologically, human beings are always either in a state of fear (contraction) or a state of love (expansion). From our habitual contractions of anxiety, dread, and apprehension emerge all the other negative emotions, such as anger, hatred, depression, confusion, foreboding, and so forth. Furthermore, when we're gripped by fear, we simply cannot feel love. Understanding this, all great religions teach that we must learn to trust God, let go of fear, live in faith, and ultimately stop worrying about the future and about death itself. No meditation program is complete that doesn't regularly turn our focus toward our emotions—especially our thoughts that generate fearful feelings—and show us how to let go of our fears through spiritual awakening, and enter into the greater state of unconditional love. Our fifth meditation will do just this.

SELF-REMEMBERING

The aim of all meditation is to become more self-aware, to remember experientially who we really are deep down. The sixth meditation specifically focuses your attention so that you are aware, at the same time, of both the outside world and your inside presence. This quality of inner-outer awareness can be directly encouraged by a special focusing meditation that leads to a sudden expansion of consciousness. The meditation is also especially valuable in maintaining a meditative state throughout your busy day, regardless of what you might be doing.

EXPERIENCING BLISS

In the first six expansions of consciousness, we progressively tune in to our breathing and set it free, let go of our worries and quiet our minds, stop judging and enter into communion with the eternal present moment, we open our hearts to our own selves, open our souls to the healing touch of our Creator—and then directly experience our own infinite presence. Then quite naturally, after having moved through those six expansions of consciousness, we enter into a state of bliss—not as a lofty idea or goal but as an actual experience. Yes, we do meditate in order to feel better, to feel absolutely blissful, on a regular basis. The final expansion encourages a total surrender to the eternal present moment—the ultimate inner act required for attaining bliss.

The Payoff

No one does anything without motivation, and meditation needs to be honestly approached with a clear understanding of the value of disciplining yourself to maintain a spiritual focus in your life. The goal of this new approach to meditation is to enable you, each and every day, to direct your full attention toward all seven of the vital qualities of life, so that you regularly shine the light of your deeper spiritual presence upon all the life themes.

The direct result of regularly turning your attention toward these meditative themes and experiences will be a beautiful awakening and reenergizing of your entire mental, emotional, and spiritual presence. Especially when you use the meditations in the order presented in this book, you'll find that you can experience a most remarkable expansion of consciousness almost every time you do the full meditation, be it in short format for two minutes or in longer formats of ten minutes, half an hour, or an hour.

What's most important is remembering to turn your full attention in each of these directions at least once a day, so that your mind, heart, and soul continually meditate upon and thus help balance and activate these seven vital dimensions of your life.

As we'll explore in depth, attention is energy, and purposefully focused attention is manifest power. Developing the mental habit of regularly focusing your mind's full meditative attention on the most important spiritual themes can transform all dimensions of your life. All you have to do is memorize and become intimately familiar with the meditations (this takes a couple of weeks at most, especially with the audio-guidance help provided) and then find time each day to move through the expansions and further awaken these dimensions of your life.

To help you integrate this meditation program into your daily life, the accompanying www.7masters.com streamed-audio and CD programs will provide you with not just one but three different meditation time frames to choose from. When you have a full half-hour, I'll guide you through a program that devotes four minutes to each of the seven expansions in turn. When you have only ten minutes, use the guided program that spends seven breaths on each of the meditations—which, as you'll find, can elicit a very deep experience.

When you have just two minutes, you'll still find it deeply rewarding to spend a short time (two breaths each) with your full being focused on each of the seven themes in turn, as you move through the seven focus phrases and gently point your total attention, however briefly . . . first to noticing your breathing . . . then to quieting your mind . . . then to accepting the world around you . . . then to loving yourself just as you are . . . then to opening your heart to receive . . . then to knowing who you really are . . . and then to experiencing fully the final breaths that leave you in present-moment bliss.

The bottom line is this: these seven meditations, however you find time to focus on them, will help you feel better and be more loving, more alert, and more harmonious and successful. As you spend time with the meditations, they will become an essential part of your every moment . . . and you will become more and more your own true self.

Experiencing Directly

Even before beginning the first chapter, let's initiate the special learning process we're going to delve into together, by exploring the simple procedure of aiming your mind's all-powerful focus of attention away from words and ideas, toward the most immediate life experience possible to a human being—that of your moment-to-moment breathing.

First of all, without any effort, become aware that right now you're focusing your mind's attention on reading these words on this page, bringing the words into your mind, and generating a sense of meaning through the flow of words. . . .

Now, while continuing to read these instructions, allow your awareness to also include the immediate sensations you're feeling *of* the air flowing in . . . and flowing out . . . your nose or mouth as you breathe. . . .

And as you remain aware of the air flowing in and out of your nose or mouth, also be aware of the breathing movements happening naturally in your chest and belly, as you breathe . . .

Say to yourself, "I'm aware of my breathing. . . ."

After reading this paragraph, you can close your eyes and continue holding your mind's focus of attention *to* your breathing . . . be open to a new experience, coming to you from the infinite spiritual potential of the present moment. . . .

FOR INSTANT STREAMED AUDIO-GUIDANCE, PLEASE GO TO
www.7masters.com

CHAPTER I

Breath Watch—Patanjali

O ne of the most curious things about human beings is that each of us possesses a vast potential for expanding our awareness in ways that bring great insight, joy, peace, and fulfillment to our lives—yet mostly we maintain our consciousness at tightly contracted levels that distance us from our deeper spiritual nature and potential.

A prime case in point is our relationship with our own breathing. It's been known for thousands of years that the simple act of being aware of our breathing can transform our lives for the better. Furthermore, there's nothing inherent in the human condition that stops us from devoting part of our awareness to our breath experience, moment to moment. We would certainly feel a whole lot better, and function at higher levels, if we gave our breathing its due attention. But even so, most of us go around with our minds entirely oblivious to our body's root source of pleasure and inspiration.

Perhaps the most fundamental psychological insight into meditation is that spiritual awakening happens only in the immediacy of the present moment. In fact, all of our human feelings and experiences happen only right here, right now. The present moment is the only place where we encounter both our inner feelings and the outside world—and nothing grounds us so deeply and immediately in the present moment as an ongoing awareness of our breath experience. This is why so many meditation traditions hold breath awareness so central in their teachings.

The primary culprit that constantly pulls our attention away from the present moment is the tendency of our thinking minds to drift away from the here and now into memories, imaginings, judgments, or abstract thought flows and reflections about those judgments. Driven by our flustered ego's constant apprehensions and ruminations, we tend to spend most of our day lost in often conflicting thoughts and emotions—problem-solving our way toward success, worrying too much about the future, planning our next business or romantic move, or perhaps daydreaming about our next vacation.

Therefore, our initial meditative challenge will be to learn ways to shift away from the past-future fixations of our thinking minds whenever we want to, and regain precious breathing space in the here and now. Linear thought flows, either in our minds or on this page, can surely inspire us and help us learn procedures that open our hearts to the meditative experience. Once we understand the meditative procedure and how to go about it, however, we'll need to put all our linear thoughts aside, and consciously redirect our focus of attention toward the present moment.

Have you noticed in your own experience how all your best moments tend to happen when you're conscious of your breathing and aware of your whole body in the here and now? This is because all human feelings gain expression through breathing. When you sigh with pleasure, for instance, you inhale and exhale deeply in passion and joy; your breathing expands and feels wonderful in your chest and belly when you feel fulfilled and content. In this chapter, we're going to learn the most effective universal meditative techniques for making your moment-to-moment breathing experience more conscious throughout your day, so that you feel more alive and "here."

Many think of meditation as something to do only when we have free time to devote exclusively to it. It's better to think of meditation as a state of consciousness we maintain every waking moment of our lives. So let's not talk about being aware of your breathing "some time in the future" when you're not doing anything else. Let's talk about being aware of your breathing every single moment—like right now, for example.

At this very moment, you're only one effortless expansion of awareness away from being on your way to the infinite inner realms of breath meditation. As you continue reading these words, simply allow your awareness to expand, without any effort at all, to also include the actual physiological sensations you're feeling right now in your nose or mouth, as the current of air you're breathing rushes in . . . and rushes out . . . and rushes in again . . .

As you continue breathing and reading at the same time, you'll realize that you don't need to change what you're doing in order to experience consciousness expansion. Nor must you make any effort to expand your consciousness to include more and more of the present moment. You can just continue reading these words and at the same time be aware of your inner breath experience.

Consciousness in its natural state loves to expand and be aware of more and more . . . until it perceives the whole. So allow the flow of these words to help you gently expand your mind's attention to also include your breathing experience . . . the sensation of the air rushing in and out your nose or mouth . . . the sensations of movement in your chest and belly as you breathe . . .

As you read these words and at the same time experience your breathing, you are already meditating. Your consciousness has expanded and will continue to expand as you stay aware of your breathing and read deeper and deeper into this book. Indeed, for the rest of your life, no matter what you're doing, you can develop this primal capacity to remain continually aware of your breathing—and thus to merge breath meditation and the rest of your life into one seamless whole.

Pause and Experience

You might want to pause a few enjoyable moments after reading this paragraph, to put the book aside . . . let go of words for a bit . . . stretch perhaps to bring your awareness to your whole body . . . and gently become a witness to your own breathing . . . tune in to the actual sensations in your nose (or mouth) being caused by the air flowing in . . . and flowing out . . . and expand your awareness to include the movements in your chest and belly as you breathe . . . give yourself permission to enjoy yourself . . . be open to a new experience . . .

Patanjali's Teachers

No one is quite sure when Patanjali was born, nor is much known about his personal life. Perhaps he lived shortly before Jesus, perhaps shortly after him. He was surely born at least a few hundred years after Buddha, because his writings and yoga teachings, most notably outlined in his famous *Yoga Sutras,* stimulated a revival of traditional Hindu yogic practice a few hundred years after Buddha's spiritual revolution. That revolution had swept India about five hundred years before Christ.

Patanjali powerfully revived the ancient yogic tradition of the Hindu culture and also brought a fast-spreading new meditative thrust to the tradition. Dozens of influential spiritual teachers would emerge in the generations after Patanjali's initial inspiration. Even today most yogic teachers ascribe their meditative roots to Patanjali, or to masters following in Patanjali's name.

However, it's important to remember that Patanjali codified and expanded on an already vast spiritual tradition dating back at least two thousand years before he wrote the *Yoga Sutras*. India and the surrounding regions were almost certainly the birthplace of the world meditative tradition.

Imagine a spiritually (not materially) focused culture in which most of the brilliant minds of each new generation, for hundreds of generations, accepted as their primary occupation the challenge of observing, from the inside out, the inner workings of the human mind and body, spirit and soul. When we tap the ancient Hindu meditative tradition, we're accessing the accumulated discoveries and wisdom of hundreds of thousands of brilliant and devout human beings who devoted their lives to looking inward, employing the tool of consciousness itself, and then sharing with each other and posterity what they discovered.

As we tap this yogic tradition in our exploration of breath meditation, we're accessing the most complete study of the breath phenomenon ever conducted. We're also participating in this ongoing research into what happens when the power and light of human consciousness are regularly focused on the most rhythmic act of the human body.

The Ins and Outs of Breathing

In his teachings, Patanjali ranged from the most obvious (yet vital) aspects of breathing to the most sublime. Indeed, toward the end of his *Yoga Sutras* he ventures into some of the most revolutionary mystic teachings in the world meditative tradition.

To begin at the beginning, Patanjali first suggests that you observe the breath experience keenly by noticing specifically:

1. when you are breathing in (inhalation);

2. when you are breathing out (exhalation); and

3. when you are temporarily holding your breath (suspension).

As he wrote in *The Yoga Sutras:* "Observing each of these three phases as they naturally occur in space and time, you can learn to make your breathing more harmonious."

Pranayama breathing as taught in traditional yogic training involves concentrating your awareness fully on each of the three phases of the breath experience in turn. By observing more closely the particulars of the inhale, the exhale, and the held breath, you discover a universe of experiential subtlety in each.

In Pranayama training you also develop the ability to control each of the three breath phases during meditation. As you consciously vary the ratio of how fast you inhale (your intake of oxygen) to how fast you exhale (your outflow of carbon dioxide), you can quickly change your energetic state.

Patanjali, following the ancient yogic formula for breath control, called the inhalation by the Sanskrit term *puraka,* the held breath by the term *kumbhaka,* and the exhalation by the term *rechaka.* Let's look a moment at each of these primal qualities of breath awareness.

THE INHALE: PURAKA

As you continue reading, for your next few breaths notice especially your inhales ... notice how the air flows in through your nose and esophagus, notice how your stomach relaxes and moves outward, your chest expands, and your upper back and rib cage move outward. . . .

The inhale is primarily a process of expansion. Your diaphragm muscle under your lungs contracts downward, and your rib cage muscles expand to create a relative vacuum inside your two lungs, thus making air from the outside come rushing into your lungs. Therefore, each inhale represents the basic expansive nature of the universe.

Pause and Experience

For the next few breaths, inhale strongly and deeply through the nose . . . feel your nostrils flare out and expand to take in more air, feel your chest expand rapidly . . . perhaps sit or stand more upright . . . notice how your mood changes when you breathe deeply and strongly . . .

THE HELD BREATH: KUMBHAKA

Kumbhaka, or held breath, occurring after the inhale or exhale is complete, consists of a deliberate stoppage of the flow of air at the top or bottom of the breath cycle and the retention of that air in the lungs for a certain amount of time, usually determined by a simple counting method.

At the top of your inhale, a short held breath enables your lungs to absorb much more oxygen. With this extra oxygen, your whole system becomes more energized and alert. Holding the breath after the exhale leads to a deeper and deeper experience of emptiness. In the Zen Buddhist tradition, the held breath after the exhale is of vital importance in letting go of "everything" and being empty on a regular basis. In our culture we tend to focus on being full, not empty. You'll find a regular meditation upon a held breath after the exhale of great liberating value.

Pause and Experience

After reading this paragraph, put the book aside and experiment with the Kumbhaka experience for a few breaths by holding your breath at the top of the inhale for a count of 2 or perhaps 4, and then for a count of 2 (or 4) at the bottom of the exhale . . . let your inhales and exhales come and go at whatever speed they naturally want to . . . observe this breathing process for perhaps eight to twelve cycles . . .

THE EXHALE: RECHAKA

The third stage of breath meditation, exhalation, is similar to the inhale in that it likes to be smooth and continuous. The exhale is very important in meditation because it reflects an emptying not only of the lungs but also of the mind.

As you become empty of air, and also of your usual thoughts and sense of self, you will often experience your ego letting go its control of your mind, allowing a unique awakening-rebirth experience that comes on the next inhale. You can also use a focus on the exhale to breathe out your emotional tensions as you empty yourself of negative feelings and then experience refreshment with the next inhale.

Pause and Experience

After reading this paragraph, put away the book for a few moments and experiment for a few breaths as you focus on long relaxed exhales . . . and also hold the breath at the bottom of each exhale . . . see what it's like to move toward emptiness . . . and then be empty of air . . . empty of thought . . . empty of yourself . . . before the next inhale comes . . .

Breathing Patterns

I'm not a great fan of relying too much on controlled breathing routines, because our primary aim is to set your breathing free, not to overly control it. But I do highly value breath control when used in moderation. Such control for a few minutes at a time in the beginning of a meditation session can rapidly break your breathing out of emotional constrictions and thus set you free.

The primary yogic technique for defining a particular breathing pattern is to count up to a certain number on the inhale, and then count again on the held breath, and again on the exhale. For instance, you might choose to inhale to the count of 2, hold for the count of 2, and exhale for the count of 4.

There are four primary breathing patterns in the yogic tradition. You can use them in any meditation to move beyond tense breathing and establish a deeper breath cycle.

BALANCING THE BREATH

A basic aim with breath control is to balance the inhale and the exhale. This seemingly simple act will quickly generate deep reverberations throughout your being. The most common way to balance the breathing is to inhale for a count of 4, then exhale for a count of 4, and repeat this pattern for at least twelve breath cycles—so that you fully calm and balance inhale and exhale.

You can also say "puraka . . . rechaka . . . puraka . . . rechaka . . ." rather than count, if you prefer. It's up to you to find the best speed for counting. You're always in charge of pacing your own breathing.

Give this simple Pranayama breathing experience a try, for eight breath cycles:

Inhale for 4 counts . . . exhale for 4 counts . . . and repeat.

HELD-BREATH BALANCING

In the Hindu yogic tradition, great emphasis is placed not just on watching the breath as it comes and goes, but on purposefully controlling your breathing so as to induce particular mental and physical states. To accomplish this, you simply change the numbers in your breath meditation.

For instance, another variation on balancing the breath is to include short held points (kumbhaka) at the top and bottom of your breathing cycle. These "still points" will greatly change your breath meditation, creating momentary experiences of total unmoving in your breathing.

> See how this one feels. Be sure to vary your pace so that it's comfortable:

> > Inhale for 4 counts . . . hold for 2 . . . exhale for 4 . . . hold for 2.

Alertness Breathing

If you want to charge yourself up with oxygen and increase your alertness, the following breath control pattern is quite powerful. You inhale deeply and slowly . . . hold for quite a while . . . exhale rapidly and hold for a short time . . . and then repeat this cycle over and over, paying full attention to your experience. Try it for six to ten breaths for a starter, and begin to make friends with this alertness breath meditation:

> Take some time to explore this pattern and discover how it feels from the inside out.

> > Inhale for 6 counts . . . hold for 4 . . . exhale for 2 . . . hold for 2.

CALMING BREATHING

Conversely, if you want to calm yourself down rapidly, inhale rapidly, hold just a little while, exhale long and slowly, and hold for quite a while. Go ahead and experiment with the effects of this pattern by going through the calming breath cycle six to ten times:

> Inhale for 2 counts . . . hold for 2 . . . exhale for 6 . . . hold for 4.

Walking the Path

Until recent centuries, almost all human beings walked or ran a considerable distance every day, and this has perhaps been the primary time for meditation. To awaken our sense of who we are, it's important, whenever possible, to get out and walk every day—and also to turn that simple act of ambulation into the sublime experience of walking meditation.

The Buddha spoke succinctly about the value of walking meditation: "These are the five rewards for one who practices walking meditation . . . He can endure traveling by foot; he can endure exertion; he becomes free from disease; whatever he has eaten and drunk, chewed and savored, becomes well-digested; and the concentration he wins while doing walking meditation lasts for a long time."

To demonstrate that we can meditate anywhere and while doing anything, Buddha pointed out that there are only four kinds of meditation: meditation done sitting upright, meditation done lying down on your back, meditation done standing in one place, and meditation done while walking. The transformation of everyday walking (and jogging as well) into a meditative practice has always been a spiritual tradition.

A walking meditation is obviously a breathing meditation because the breath becomes quite central when exercising. There are a number of walking meditation traditions, some complex, some utterly simple. I prefer very simple walking meditations. Let me teach you the one I do most often in its several variations. Drawn from the yogic tradition of Patanjali, it's both very easy and utterly profound.

PURAKA-RECHAKA WALKING MEDITATION

As you're walking, begin to be aware of your natural breathing rhythm. Feel the air rushing into and out of your nose or mouth, and your chest and belly working to bring plenty of air into your lungs.

Once you're focused deeply on your breathing and settled into your general pace, breathe through the mouth and begin to whisper "rechaka" as you exhale and on your inhale whisper "puraka." You can say these words either quietly, even subliminally, or fairly loud.

Now expand your awareness to include the sensations in your feet as you walk. When you expand your awareness to include two or more things at once, you effectively quiet the thoughts flowing through your mind, and move into a clear state of consciousness. You're aware of your whole body and spiritual presence at once, without any thoughts at all. I encourage you to practice this puraka-rechaka walking meditation every day as a vital aspect of your breath-watch meditation.

STEP-COUNT WALKING MEDITATION

When you're out walking, notice how many steps you naturally take for each inhale and for each exhale. You'll probably find that you're taking two, three, or four steps for each inhale, and the same for each exhale. Now, start counting your steps on the inhale, and then on the exhale, so that you set up a simple chant of "One two three . . . one two three" or perhaps "One two . . . one two." The act of saying these numbers to yourself will serve gently to quiet all other thoughts running through your mind.

Pause and Experience

I encourage you to get up wherever you are right now, while this is fresh in your mind, and begin to master this simple meditation by walking down the hallway or around the room. Start walking and counting your steps . . . and notice how almost immediately this rhythmic action and whispered vocalization shifts you into a more peaceful, alert, enjoyable state of mind and being. . . .

Acquiring Your Seat

You know naturally what physical position to assume when you are walking. But how about when you want to sit down and meditate? Is there a "correct" way to sit in meditation, or can you just slouch down however you want and attain optimum results?

Yogic masters have a great deal to say about "acquiring your seat," as they put it. Patanjali offers an utterly simple statement about posture for meditation: "The posture is firm and soft." In other words, you need to be firm in muscle tone so as to hold your body upright against the pull of gravity, yet you need to also be relaxed, which is accomplished by being balanced so that you exert minimal effort in remaining upright.

The challenge I offer you in the next weeks and months is to experiment with different ways of sitting, so that you can be comfortable for a period of time, with enough muscle tone to hold you upright, and yet be fully relaxed in your posture as well, so that you're exerting minimum effort to remain upright.

In the *Anapanasati* breath-meditation Sutra of the Buddha, he offers the following suggestion:

> "The meditator, having gone to the forest, to the shade of a tree, or to an empty building, sits down with legs folded crosswise, body held erect, and sets mindfulness to the fore. Always mindful, the meditator breathes in; mindful, the meditator breathes out."

And now, specifically how to sit? Buddha, in harmony with the ancient tradition of yogic discipline from which he emerged, recommends sitting "with legs folded crosswise, body held erect." In one of the very best contemporary commentaries on breathing, *Breath by Breath*, Larry Rosenberg expands on this short suggestion to make it more relevant to Western meditators. In place of the traditional cross-legged posture, "Some people in the West accomplish the same thing with a kneeling posture using a cushion or a bench, or by sitting in a chair. The key factors are comfort and stability. The simple act of sitting in a stable upright posture with calmness and dignity has an importance of its own."

Beyond Shoulds and Shouldn'ts

If you're new to meditation and haven't yet experimented with finding your optimum meditative posture, I recommend that instead of trying to force yourself to sit according to some external standard of classic meditation, you discipline yourself only to the extent of sitting cross-legged or on a straight-back chair for five minutes or more at a time. Rather than approach the meditative process with too many notions about "shoulds" and "proper procedures" from the tradition, just sit and observe what you naturally do.

After all, the aim of meditation isn't to make yourself sit still or to hold a particular posture. The aim of meditation is to expand your consciousness, to become fully aware of the present moment, to awaken your attention to your own deeper being. You can slouch in line at McDonald's and still be meditating—as long as you're doing your best to remain focused on your breathing and your whole-body presence. Whenever you're holding your attention to the here and now and perceiving your inner and outer reality without judging it, you're meditating.

By freeing yourself from the idea that meditation requires a particular posture, you also set yourself free to meditate while commuting, while sitting in your office chair, while reclining in the backyard or at the beach. I often relax to read for an hour or so in my easy chair after a long day, and I love to take just five to ten minutes in that utterly relaxed position to meditate. There's really no reason not to pause regularly in whatever position you find yourself, even standing on a subway train, say to yourself the focus statements with each new breath, and instantly shift into meditation mode.

Of course, you will find that the sitting-upright position does tend to help your meditation deepen most rapidly. Almost everyone, when they set themselves free to assume whatever posture they want, spontaneously make a lot of movements at first, as they set their bodies free to move as they want to. But ultimately, their body will realize that sitting upright requires the least energy and balancing attention. They will find themselves sitting exactly as the Buddha suggested, not because they made themselves sit properly according to someone else's dictates, but because they discovered on their own, their own seat.

This is the heart of a true meditation process—minimal external "shoulds" and "shouldn'ts" and maximum room to experiment and explore and discover. You will find on your own the essential process of meditation, as it relates to your unique personality and life flow. You will become "straight and comfortable, relaxed and balanced," because it feels good to sit that way, and because when you set your body free, it progresses naturally to that discovery.

Mindfulness to the Fore

When you're finally sitting in a posture at least somewhat comfortable and upright, what do you do next? Patanjali and his entire yogic tradition recommend that you bring "mindfulness to the fore." Mindfulness is a long word much touted in religious and self-help circles these days, but don't be intimidated by it. The term means simply "being aware of what's happening in the present moment." If you're thinking, be aware that you're thinking. If you're breathing, be aware that you're breathing. If you're walking, be aware that you're walking. That's being mindful.

Mindfulness means being aware of what you're experiencing in your environment and, at the same time, being aware of yourself as the experiencer. So when you're sitting, be aware of your sitting and of everything else that's happening in the present moment. Especially in the beginning of your meditation session you can follow the Buddha's recommendation: "Always mindful, the meditator breathes in; mindful, the meditator breathes out."

Pause and Explore

Take some time here to explore for yourself how different postures change your experience of your breath watch. After reading this paragraph, put the book aside for a while and let your body move through its changes as it explores various postures for meditating on your breathing. Feel free to do whatever you want to do—sit on the floor, move to another chair—to begin to find your own meditative seat.

The Three Pillars

Thus far we've been using the term "meditation" in its broadest generic meaning to refer to the mental process of consciously directing your mind so as to focus your attention in directions that encourage spiritual peace, clarity, and awakening. Let me share with you another set of insights from the *Yoga Sutras* and the Hindu tradition, where the three primary dimensions to the meditative practice are called *concentration, contemplation,* and *deep meditation.* In this more advanced understanding, "meditation" refers specifically to the third and final stage of the three-stage process.

CONCENTRATION

Patanjali says early in his *Yoga Sutras* that "yoga is the ability to direct and focus mental activity. . . . Concentration is focusing the mind on a particular object. With the attainment of a focused mind, the inner being establishes itself in all its reality. Otherwise, one identifies with the activities of the mind. . . . Control over the mind's fluctuations comes from persevering practice, which is the effort to attain and maintain the state of mental peace."

In the three-phase understanding of meditation that Patanjali presents, you begin by employing your will power (discipline) to concentrate your mind's full attention on your breathing in the present moment. In this state of concentration, you focus on your chosen sensory input over a period of time, returning your awareness to your breath experience when it tends to drift away. As a further aid to concentrating in the direction you want, you can say to yourself, "I'm breathing freely."

Pause and Experience

To experience your own power to concentrate, close your eyes and turn your focus to the physical sensations being generated by your breathing. Feel the air flowing in . . . feel the air flowing out . . . when your attention drifts, gently but firmly bring it back to its chosen focus on your breathing . . .

CONTEMPLATION

When you concentrate on the immediate sensations of your breath experience, you'll discover that your habitual thought flows tend to quiet down. Your mind will become centered on your chosen theme (your breathing in this case), and often you'll intuitively begin to reflect—intellectually, emotionally, and symbolically—on the underlying nature of your breathing. This is where concentration shifts into contemplation, the second step of spiritual focusing.

The Christian contemplative tradition, for instance, often suggests reflecting on a saying from the Bible through deep contemplation, which may result in sudden insight into the deeper meaning of the words. In Hindu practice, the light of a candle might be the focus of contemplation, or the nature of water, or one's breathing, as seen from every possible point of view. When Jesus asked his disciples and followers to "consider the lilies, and how they grow," he was suggesting that they contemplate the deeper spiritual nature of the lilies and plumb the depths of meaning that often emerge through such contemplation.

The focus phrase for each meditation will often in and of itself stimulate contemplation. "I am breathing freely" will lead to a primal reflection on what it means to be free, and to breathe freely as opposed to controlling the breath.

Pause and Reflect

Let's pause again and experience directly the mental process of contemplation. Tune in to your own breathing . . . say to yourself, "I'm breathing freely," . . . and reflect on what it really means to breathe freely . . . notice that after your next exhale, if you hold your breath, at some point a subtle inner power will spark a new inhale. Experience this breath reflex that keeps you alive . . . see how deeply you can look to the source of that reflex as you observe the power that is compelling you to breathe. What power is it, and where does it come from?

DEEP MEDITATION

After concentrating on and then contemplating your breathing, your mind will naturally reach the end of its inquiry, at least for now, and become quiet. This shift into total inner quiet and cessation of inquiry initiates entry into the third dimension of spiritual focusing, deep meditation.

This experience begins when we quiet all the ideas and emotions associated with whatever we're focusing on, and move beyond conceptual consciousness altogether . . . into a state of awareness where we're simply alive in the present moment and at one with the focus of our attention. We watch without judging, and experience what it means to be conscious beyond our thinking minds.

In this state we effortlessly experience the merger of our personal awareness with the greater awareness, and enter into true communion with the divine beyond all concepts.

What is the boundary between contemplation and meditation? As we're using the term here, contemplation is a mental and intuitive inquiry into the nature of your chosen focal point, using cognitive association and reasoning, memory, imagination, and intuitive reflection to explore it. Meditation is the experience of the mind when the cognitive function becomes quiet, when associations with the past and future fall away and you become fully conscious in expanded awareness of the present moment.

Over the next days, months, and years, it's important to devote considerable time to contemplation, because it allows the thinking mind to play a part in the process of enlightenment. From my understanding, spiritual awakening is ultimately not a process of controlling the mind but of setting it free. In the process of setting it free, you also remain deeply observant of what the mind does, moment to moment . . . watching everything that happens in the mind . . . and as you observe how the mind's attention drifts here or there, how it contemplates this or that theme or object or feeling, the flash of realization comes that takes you beyond . . .

The spiritual teacher Osho says it this way:

> A man has to learn only one thing—a single step and the journey is over. That single step is to do everything watchfully. Start watching your mind, your body, your actions. Don't lose the watcher—then it doesn't matter whether you are a Christian or a Hindu or a Buddhist. A man who can do everything fully consciously becomes a luminous phenomenon.

Pause and Experience

Just watch the present moment unfolding . . . experience everything that comes to your awareness . . . sounds . . .

sights . . . sensations . . . smells . . . thoughts . . . emotions . . .
touch . . . movement . . . make no effort . . . don't evaluate or
judge or reflect . . . simply be the observer . . . the witness . . .

Freeing the Breath

We've now seen some of the great gifts that the yogic tradition
of Patanjali has given us for walking the universal path of
meditation. We must always start our meditations, as Patanjali and
the yogic tradition tell us, by choosing to focus our attention in particular directions and in particular ways that will prove worthwhile
spiritually, especially toward the breath experience.

This tradition is also very much concerned with discipline, effort,
and control as a prerequisite for the more liberated meditation experiences. A certain amount of discipline is required on the spiritual
path, no matter what tradition or approach one chooses to explore.

The key focus phrase for this chapter and meditation, however,
is not "I am breathing in a controlled manner," or "I am disciplining my breathing," but rather, "I am breathing freely."

In yogic meditation, a primary aim is to attain total control of
all of one's physical, mental, and emotional activities, inclinations,
habits, and reflexes. The yogic tradition cites many good reasons
for placing discipline and effort at the center of your spiritual practice, which I experienced myself while going through this training
for several years under the tutelage of Yogananda's disciple
Kriyananda.

At the same time, however, I was exploring meditation with
Alan Watts and other Zen teachers, and learning the great value of
approaching my breathing in just the opposite direction of control—that of setting the breathing entirely free.

At a certain point I suddenly understood the value of the insights that Buddha brought to the Indian spiritual tradition, especially his insistence that to simply observe the breath experience without any control whatsoever is the most powerful way to move into deep meditation.

In our *Seven Masters* approach to meditation, after benefiting from the yogic insights into disciplining the mind to begin our meditation, we rapidly move beyond such discipline—and set our breathing free. In this spirit, during the first guided breath meditation, I'll include just enough initial self-discipline so that you purposefully take control of your mind's power of attention and aim it in rewarding spiritual directions—in this case toward your breathing experience. I'll also offer a bit of controlled breathing as we share together in the benefits of the puraka-kumbhaka-rechaka breath control techniques.

Then I'll encourage you to let go of all control—except for the general continued focusing of your attention on your breathing—so that you can observe your breaths coming and going without in any way controlling them.

Awakening or Enlightenment

In similar vein, meditation is often understood as a goal-oriented effort that is aimed at some time in the distant future, toward the attainment of an ultimate state of totally transcendent consciousness called enlightenment.

I'd like to clarify that this book and set of meditations are not aimed at pushing you toward that distant future goal of becoming a fully enlightened being. These meditations don't approach the spiritual path as a linear progression of meditative achievement toward a future goal. The focus here is on experiencing in the present moment the ongoing process of spiritual awakening, rather than dreaming of attaining some distant ideal state of enlightenment.

In reality, spiritual awakening never happens off in the future. It happens only right here, right now, even as you continue reading these words and are aware of your breathing at the same time, you're experiencing spiritual awakening. The process of walking the spiritual path is, in and of itself, the awakening.

Every chapter and every meditation expansion in this book is designed to encourage you to make the leap into realizing that right here, right now, with absolutely no further training or discipline or learning, you are already here. Just pay attention and look and you will see.

The Zen folk say, "Nowhere to go, nothing to do." All you have to do is wake up to the reality that you are an enlightened being by nature. And to wake up, all you have to do is pay attention to the ongoing, miraculous unfolding of the eternal present moment.

As Ram Dass has chanted continually, we have nothing to do except "be here now." Alan Watts explored the same realization in his book with the unequivocal title *This Is It*. The kingdom of heaven is indeed at hand.

So let's not waste any time thinking about or preparing for our future enlightenment. Let's just give ourselves permission to wake up, . . . right now.

BREATH WATCH: Guided Meditation 1

Let me guide you through our first formal consciousness-expansion process, the breath-watch meditation you've been learning piece by piece in this chapter. In its full form, and with the primary pacing offered on the audio-guidance session you'll find on the Internet or CD, this meditation moves you through seven to eight minutes of inner experience. Once you've memorized this process, you can either take longer with it or move more rapidly through a shortened form of it.

What's important is that through the discipline of regularly turning your attention to your breathing, you begin to develop the spiritual habit of being aware of your breathing more and more often, wherever you are and whatever you're doing. The aim is to learn to remain aware of your breathing throughout much of each day, allowing a deep, meditative quality of consciousness to permeate your daily routine and life.

For those of you who want to hear me guide you through the process, rather than reading and memorizing the process on your own (either way is fine!), please go to www.7masters.com for instant streamed-audio guidance.

> To begin this breath-watch meditation, just make yourself comfortable, preferably in an upright sitting position, or perhaps lying on your back or standing upright. Allow yourself to relax and get comfortable . . . and without doing anything at all, just begin to notice how you feel in your body . . . let your mind roam here and there freely . . . and notice if your breathing feels tense or relaxed . . . uneven or smooth . . . don't judge your breathing, just observe it . . .
>
> Be sure to give yourself permission to make any bodily movements that spontaneously want to happen . . . set yourself free to move your head . . . arms and hands . . . and torso . . . this way and that . . . breathe through the mouth a few times perhaps . . . stretch if that feels good . . . raise your hands into the air . . . yawn perhaps, with a good deep sigh . . .
>
> And now just relax . . . begin to settle into a comfortable balanced position as you effortlessly acquire your seat for meditation . . . breathing freely . . . feeling what your spine wants to do . . . finding a balanced posture that feels good for your meditation . . .
>
> You can now turn your attention again to your breathing . . . bring your focus to the tip of your nose and the inner lining of your nose . . . feel the actual sensation in your nose or mouth, as you breathe, of the air flowing in . . . and flowing out . . . .

And now, at the same time, expand your awareness, as you breathe, to include the movements you feel in your chest and your belly . . .

Now, for a couple of minutes, let's practice Pranayama balanced breathing . . . inhaling for 4 counts . . . holding for 2 counts . . . exhaling for 4 counts . . . and holding for 2 counts . . . inhale again for 4 counts . . . hold for 2 counts . . . exhale for 4 counts . . . hold for 2 counts . . . again inhale for 4 counts . . . hold for 2 counts . . . exhale for 4 counts . . . hold for 2 counts . . . continue with this Pranayama breathing on your own . . .

Okay, now you can just set your breathing free . . . let the inhales and exhales come on their own . . . allow your breathing to stop whenever it wants, and start when it wants . . . just watch your breathing, without in any way interfering with its natural effortless flow and movement . . . *just* hold your attention on the air flowing in . . . and out . . . your nose or mouth . . . and at the same time on the movements in your chest and belly as you breathe.

Say to yourself, "I am breathing freely." And for the next few minutes, if you want to, you can reflect on what it means to breathe . . . contemplate your breathing experience from all points of view . . . inquire into what it means to regularly make these movements . . . to be a breather . . .

And now, when you're ready, you can move into the enlightening quietness of deep meditation, as you focus on your breath coming in, going out . . . free.

FOR INSTANT STREAMED-AUDIO GUIDANCE, PLEASE GO TO
www.7masters.com

CHAPTER 2

Quieting the Mind—Lao Tzu

There's nothing deeper in meditation than mastering the process of quieting our thoughts and entering into a state of inner quiescence. If we could only calm our chronic chattering minds at will, there would be no need for formal meditative practice at all.

There's of course nothing wrong with thinking per se—as long as we don't become constantly bombarded with thoughts, with no periods of mental quiet to refresh our spirits. What meditation offers is a healthy balance between the busy-ness of nonstop thinking, and the inner peace and clarity of a quiet mind.

In this chapter, I'll encourage you to begin to observe as often you can the thoughts that keep springing to mind. Are they thoughts that make you feel good, that encourage your participation in the world, that lead to positive action? Or are your habitual thought flows more focused on worries, on judgmental criticisms, on antagonisms and conflicts?

The raw truth psychologically is that most of us spend far too much time each day lost in negative thoughts that directly stimulate inner emotions such as anger, anxiety, depression, confusion, and all the rest. And the combination of these thoughts and emotions tends to wreak havoc with our lives, generating stress-related health problems, relationship conflicts, difficulties at work, and inner confusion and torment in our souls.

You'll find that almost every time you decide to pause and meditate, be it for two minutes, twenty minutes, or two hours, you bring to your meditation a loud pushy assortment of thoughts that want to continue to dominate your mind. Thoughts of the joyful, positive, loving kind are usually very happy to quiet down so that you can enter into deep meditation. However, worried or tormented thoughts tend to refuse to let up or to give you any peace of mind. Your internal ego voice will insist that there's no time to stop worrying and scheming, that it's vital for you to keep thinking in order to solve a problem, to make important plans, to stay immersed in your inner conceptual world—rather than stop thinking and focus on the experiential world of the present moment.

Several thousands of years ago, among the wise folk in the Taoist culture of ancient China, the judging, analytical thinking mind was already correctly identified as the perpetrator not only of our particularly human blessings in life, but also of our particularly human curses. They understood clearly that by dwelling in thoughts grounded in memory, imagination, beliefs, and assumptions, we humans have gained vast powers to think logically, reflect upon past experiences, and manipulate the world to our advantage. However, because thinking is a past-future function of the mind, we have tended to lose touch with the vital experience of participating spontaneously in the present moment.

Meditation aims to resolve this "lost in thought" dilemma as we temporarily distance ourselves from the constant barrage of thoughts from our inner virtual reality, and shift into a deeper consciousness. By learning to calmly watch thoughts flowing through our minds without being attached to those thoughts, we liberate ourselves from chronic identification with our ego's limited notion of what life is all about and open ourselves to deeper spiritual wisdom, insight, and nurturing. By quieting the dominant thinking mind, we awaken our latent spiritual consciousness; by gaining release from our worries and mental torments, enjoy life more fully.

In the Taoist tradition, when we quiet our thoughts in meditation, we let go of trying to manipulate the world based on our inner fantasies of how things should be. We attain a humble sense of peace simply by observing and responding directly to what's happening in the always new present moment.

The Reluctant Sage

Lao Tzu was born in southern China in the state of Ch'u, now known as the Hunan Province, around 2,500 years ago—one hundred years or so before Buddha was born over the big hill, in India. Living a very quiet life, Lao Tzu would enter posterity with only one noticeable accomplishment—the writing of a thin volume of spiritual reflections called the *Tao Te Ching*, which has since been published in more languages than any book except the Bible.

This remarkable book's writer was not at all famous during his long lifetime, which some records indicate was well over a hundred years. We know very little of his daily life except that in early adulthood he moved to Loyang and served as custodian of the Imperial Archives of the Chou House for at least fifty years. He worked in the emperor's library, kept mostly to himself, and was considered a recluse and a mystic of deep wisdom. All during his long tenure at the Imperial Archives he wrote (to our knowledge) absolutely nothing, nor did he allow any disciples to gather around him.

We do know, from the writings of Chuang Tzu, the greatest Taoist teacher after Lao Tzu, that the venerable philosopher Confucius (who was born a generation after Lao Tzu) once sought out Lao Tzu for an interview, during which Lao Tzu told the soon-to-be famous philosopher and moralist: "Strip yourself of your proud airs and numerous desires, your complacent demeanor and excessive ambitions. They won't do you any good. This is all I have to say to you."

Following this now-famous interview with the old man, young Confucius said to his disciples, "I don't know how dragons can ride upon the wind and clouds and soar to high heaven. I saw Lao Tzu today. He can be likened to a dragon."

As far as we can determine, Lao Tzu lived a simple contemplative life in which he learned step by step how to practice what he understood to be "the Way" or "the Path"—or in Chinese, the Tao. It seems that throughout his life he walked his walk but didn't much talk any talk. According to Henry Wei, in his excellent book *Lao Tzu: The Guiding Light:*

> Lao Tzu may rightly be regarded as an immortal inspirer. His teachings constitute a bright beacon for the guidance of the human spirit to supreme fulfillment. . . . He led a long, quiet and studious life and then vanished from the human scene, leaving behind a compact parcel of sublime wisdom in glorious poetry. . . . He was not exactly a hermit or recluse, but simply loved the contemplative life. He preferred to stay in obscurity in the silence of the library, devoting himself to inner culture and the pursuit of truth, living with serene spontaneity and natural ease.

The empire that Lao Tzu served, the House of Chou, was falling into decadence and decline. Finally the old man had had enough of the city and decided to take his leave. He simply started walking westward, heading toward the distant mountain pass. Arriving at the gate leading out of the Chou empire, he was halted by the keeper of the border, a man named Yin Hsi, who asked of him, "Before you retire entirely from the world, will you please write some words for our enlightenment?"

Lao Tzu obviously agreed, because before he walked out

through the gates and disappeared into another kingdom and who-knows-what personal life experience, he left with Yin Hsi a slender collection of eighty-one short poems and reflections, consisting in total of only around five thousand words.

Taoism in general received a great jolt from Lao Tzu's powerful teachings. He was a truly revolutionary thinker who directly challenged the status quo and lauded humble human qualities that anyone could aspire to; he measured greatness not in wealth and accomplishments but in personal integrity and inner harmony. From the *Tao Te Ching*'s teachings, it's clear that he was in favor of leaders supporting the welfare of the people, and entirely against war, violence, official corruption, exorbitant taxation, and all undue interference in the life of the community. He posited an ideal leadership that was invisible and enlightened, knowing firsthand the deeper spiritual path to governing. Ever since, astute statesmen and leaders in all positions have cherished his insights and guidance.

The Greater Reality

The *Tao Te Ching* regularly points our attention toward our natural capacity for transcendence. A unique gift of the Taoist tradition is that it does not see transcendent experience as separate and "other" but fully integrates inner and outer, everyday and mystic, pragmatic and transcendent. The Tao is a path we can all readily follow without fears of falling over some esoteric edge, because the Tao points directly to everyday reality and says, right here before you, in your everyday routine, you will find transcendence—you will encounter the Tao.

Through his remarkable scholastic efforts and intuitive insights into the *Tao Te Ching,* Henry Wei has delineated six primary features of meditation, as clarified by Lao Tzu and his followers, that lead to mystic realization. These steps or qualities are strong indicators that point us toward a spiritual path we can follow all our lives.

You'll surely notice how similar this book's meditation program is to the insights and guidelines of Lao Tzu and the Taoist tradition. Indeed, the mystic path, by its very nature, is a universal path, informed not by intellectual ruminations and differentiations but by the common inner experience that comes to all of us when we turn our attention in certain directions, and open our hearts and souls to the greater reality.

STEP 1: CONCENTRATION ON THE CENTER

Lao Tzu's first step toward mystic meditation is that of turning your mind's attention toward the center of your own being, in the act of mental concentration. The founder of Ch'an or Zen Buddhism in China, Bodhidharma, offers the following succinct guideline for meditating: "Direct pointing at the mind of man," he encourages, "seeing into one's own true nature." In this light, Lao Tzu himself asked the primary meditative question: "Can you concentrate without deviating?"

STEP 2: TENDERNESS OF BREATH

The second feature of the Taoist approach to meditation is awareness of your breathing experience. The ancient Chinese put great importance on counting your breaths during the initial phase of meditation.

However, Lao Tzu offers no guidance on breath control. He was more focused on the natural breathing process: "In attuning your breathing to induce tenderness, can you become like a newborn baby?" In other words, can you set your breathing so free that it is entirely beyond your emotional constrictions and restricted breathing habits? Can you let your breaths come and go entirely naturally?

STEP 3: CLEANSING THE MIND

Again, Lao Tzu asks one of his powerful questions: "In cleansing and purifying the Mystic Mirror, can you make it free from all stain?"

In need of purification are the chronic thoughts we allow to run through our minds that pollute and stain our experience with fears and angers and manipulatory notions that disturb our natural quiescence. When the mind becomes quiet and stops judging and manipulating and resisting the natural way, then we succeed with Lao Tzu's third feature of meditation.

STEP 4: LOVING WITHOUT INTERFERING

The fourth feature of Taoist meditation is usually called by the primal Chinese term *Wu Wei*, which refers to "the serene and effortless performance of one's daily duties," or "no willful interference in or manipulation of the natural free spontaneous course of the Tao."

Lao Tzu again asks a question to clarify his understanding of the practice in action: "In loving the people and ruling the state, can you practice non-interference?"

Throughout his teaching in the *Tao Te Ching*, he strongly advises that we nurture the spontaneous peaceful life, that we not impose our will through manipulation of aggressive emotions and actions. In this same spirit, we can approach our own inner life with a loving quality that accepts how we are without trying to change how we are, just as we rule our minds with serenity rather than with force or manipulation.

STEP 5: SURRENDERING TO THE FEMININE

The fifth aspect of mystic meditation teaches us to allow our softer, more intuitive, and less dominating feminine qualities to rise to the fore, so that we're surrendering rather than dominating, receiving rather than broadcasting, loving rather than fighting.

Again Lao Tzu asks the crucial question for the theme at hand: "When the Heavenly Gate opens and closes, can you play the party of the Female?"

This question refers to the dualistic notion of *yin* and *yang* in Chinese culture: the One is divided through the creative powers of the Tao into two opposite energetics and qualities, which then give birth to "the ten thousand things." Lao Tzu is advising that, as the Heavenly Gate opens and we enter a mystic state of consciousness, we surrender to this experience rather than try to manipulate it.

Step 6: Encouraging Balance

The sixth quality of mystic union, according to Lao Tzu, is the nurturing of perfect equanimity: "When your light shines forth in all directions, can you ignore it with perfect equanimity?"

He's speaking here of how we remain balanced and unattached when we enter into a deep spiritual state of being and our "light shines forth in all directions." This state is similar to the Transfiguration of Jesus: "After six days Jesus took Peter, James and John and brought them up to a high isolated mountain, and was transformed before them. His face shone like the sun, and his raiment was white as the light."

When we reach a high level of realization (or indeed accomplish anything in life), our challenge is to not get excited or puffed up with pride but to remain calm, humble, and in "perfect equanimity" if we want to continue in this deep state of consciousness.

Pause and Experience

As you read these words that continue flowing across the page, allow yourself to notice, without any judgment at all, whether you're still aware of your breathing experience, or whether it has dropped away . . . again move through the effortless process of becoming aware of your breathing experience . . . the air flowing in and out of your nose . . . the movements in your chest and belly as you breathe . . . and your heart, beating right in the middle of your breathing . . . experience yourself fully here in this present moment . . .

The Natural Way

In the Taoist approach to life, we observe nature (ourselves) just as it is and learn to participate without manipulation in the spontaneous unfolding of the present moment. Let's now explore how we can apply the *Wu Wei* approach to our own evolving meditation routine, in such a way as to merge the ancient wisdom with certain new cutting-edge psychology techniques that will enable us to effortlessly quiet the mind, without controlling the mind.

In Buddhist *Vipassana* meditation, the instruction for doing the meditation is very simple: simply observe your breathing and do your best to hold your mind's attention on your breath experience for perhaps half an hour or an hour at a time. It's a pure *Wu Wei* approach to meditation, and for some people it does provide adequate instruction—it points the mind's attention toward the breathing and then, as you do your best to maintain your concentration on your breathing, it lets you have total freedom to explore what happens without trying to change what happens.

This is of course easier said than done. Naturally, thoughts are going to keep pushing into your concentration on your breathing, pulling your attention off into the past and the future and away from the present moment. When this happens, you're supposed to simply observe such thoughts as they flow through your mind, without attaching to them, and then let go of them and return to the breath focus. But we all tend to drift off into thoughts again and again and again. And so we gently bring the awareness back to the breath. Again, and again.

I love this meditation and highly recommend it. You'll note that the first step in our meditation program is very similar in procedure. However, I've known many people who struggled with the *Vipassana* meditation and often finally just gave up, because their chattering minds simply wouldn't give them a break.

In meditative practice, especially at the beginning, it does sometimes seem that quieting the mind is downright impossible. However, recent psychological evidence shows the opposite. Human beings are quite capable of quieting the flow of thoughts through their minds at will. Furthermore, certain mental tricks that we can perform will effortlessly and almost immediately quiet the flow of thoughts through the mind—during formal meditation or at any other time when we want inner peace.

Cognitive Shifting

I was lucky enough a number of years ago to be at the right place at the right time to participate in seminal meditation research being conducted by Humphrey Osmond at the New Jersey Neuro-Psychiatric Research Institute. During my stay there, we made a seemingly simple discovery that has haunted me ever since. Recently, with new research in the same area, that discovery has provided a remarkable way to almost instantly quiet the flow of thoughts through the mind, without using any psychological karate at all.

For our purposes here, the key insight drawn from this research is this: when a person is thinking actively (as documented with EEG equipment) and then focuses on one perceptual happening, such as a sound, a tactile sensation, or an image, the brain waves remain basically the same and thoughts continue to flow through the mind. We can expand our mind's attention to include one perceptual input and still keep thinking actively without losing our concentration on our thoughts.

However, researchers have discovered that when the human mind focuses on two distinct sensory inputs at the same time (a sound and an image, for instance, or breath and heartbeat), all thoughts almost immediately stop flowing through the mind. The thinking machine can be purposefully short-circuited simply by focusing on two distinct perceptual inputs at the same time.

You can learn about additional research on this discovery through updates. You've already been in training for putting this psychological insight into action. As soon as you focus on both the sensation of air flowing in and out of your nose and, at the same time, the movements in your chest and belly as you breathe, you've shifted into this expanded state where chronic thoughts tend to stop.

The scientific premise at play here is that, when you're thinking, you're continually focused on a point, performing what's called in cognitive psychology the act of "point fixation." Thinking is a matter of focusing your attention in a linear manner on one word or phrase or sentence at a time, and then shifting your focus of attention to the next word or phrase or sentence. That's exactly what you're doing as you read these words. Thinking is very much a function of linear, step-by-step point fixation. For much of each day we're absorbed in this process—focusing our attention on a particular point in space, or a particular series of words running through our minds, one after the other. This is called linear deductive thinking—point after point.

When you shift your focus of attention to include two things at the same time, you entirely change your focusing system from point fixation, to space fixation.

Experiment by looking at these two different points in space printed below. Look at one point at a time, shifting back and forth. Then see what happens when you look in such a way as to take in both points at the same time.

❋   ❋

When you shift from seeing one point at a time to seeing both of them at once, something utterly basic and even transcendent happens in the mind. When your mind shifts to look at the whole at once rather than at one point at a time, you're shifting from a mundane to a mystic level of consciousness.

Consider this universal example. When you look out the window or walk outside and suddenly come face-to-face with a magnificent sunset and are overwhelmed by the experience, notice carefully—are you busy looking at one point of the sunset at a time, then shifting your attention to focus to another point of the sunset? No, of course not. You're struck by the beauty of the sunset when you suddenly let go of point fixation and stare at the sunset in such a way that you take in the whole at once. That shift in mental focusing, not just the visual presence of the sunset, is what suddenly shifts you into a transcendent state.

You'll find that it's the same whenever you encounter something beautiful and are momentarily overwhelmed with mystic awe, be it a flower or a song. You don't look at your lover's face point by point when you're swooning in passion. Rather, you shift into "seeing the whole at once" with your gaze while making love—and thus activate an inner experience entirely different from point fixation.

Please don't take my word for this. As Krishnamurti said over and over, look for yourself to find out what is true.

The Mystic Gaze

Here's another experiment for exercising your ability to expand into mystic realms of consciousness at will and almost instantly. Let's discover the difference between staring at one point, shifting to gaze at two points, and then gazing at three points all at once.

1. First of all, with point fixation, look from one point to another, concentrating your mind's attention strongly on one point at a time. Move around the triangle three or four times, experiencing the shifting in your mind.

2. Now, become aware of your breathing as you do this, and with each breath, shift your visual attention from one point to another so that you are concentrating meditatively on each point. You'll notice that by including your breathing in your awareness you're already moving in the direction of an expanded experience.

3. While remaining deeply attuned to your breathing, shift your focus to include the top two points at once, and breathe into this experience . . . notice how your awareness of the space between you and the paper suddenly pops into being as you expand to include two things at once.

4. Now shift your focus to include all three dots at once . . . and be open to a subtle mystic experience where you have transcended all linear thinking and perception and are aware of the One.

You almost surely found out for yourself that, in order to see everything at once, your eyes must turn slightly inward and focus not right at the surface of the page but a few inches in front of it. This is what it means to "gaze" at something: you let go of a tight focus on a point, and instead focus your mind's attention somewhere in front of what you're looking at. You shift into a new dimension that includes space and volume. Everything will become a bit softer as you suddenly leave the flatness of two-dimensional space (point fixation) and enter three-dimensional space (space fixation).

As you make this primal shift, you'll sense that you're letting go of a certain control. Point fixation is very masculine—it's about pinpointing, about getting your finger on it. With space fixation, or seeing everything at once, you let go of such control, surrender to the whole, and become more feminine—just as Lao Tzu recommends.

Breathing Space

Spiritual awakening is often talked about in terms of consciousness expansion. Very often we go around living our lives locked away in just two dimensions. It's vital to understand that whenever we're thinking—which is most of the time—we're existing in a two-dimensional linear world that has no depth or space.

Thinking, by its nature, is clearly two-dimensional. Even when you focus on your breathing right where it first touches the tip of your nose, you're still having a mostly two-dimensional experience with no depth or volume or space.

Then, when you expand your awareness to include both your nose breathing and your chest breathing, something remarkable happens inside your mind—you suddenly experience yourself as having volume! This first expansion is every bit as wonderful as all future expansions of consciousness, because going from flat to volume is a vast burst of consciousness into true three-dimensional space. And it's a radical expansion that you can experience anytime you want just by doing the simple breath meditation you've already learned.

If you want to experience consciousness expansion every day, tapping your mystic potential to keep in touch with your deeper self, just remember to begin your meditation with techniques that shift your awareness beyond the two-dimensional realms of thought fixation, into three-dimensional space fixation. Each time you do this you feel yourself suddenly coming alive again.

Pause and Experience

Since practice makes perfect, and experience is what we thrive on spiritually, let's move through this process again. After reading this paragraph and putting the book aside, relax and turn your attention to the air flowing in and out through your nose or mouth. Focus fully on that point where the air enters your nose . . . notice whether any thoughts continue flowing through your mind . . . and then expand your awareness to include both the air flowing through your nose and the movements in your chest and belly as you breathe . . . feel the sudden sense of expansion, the volume of your body . . . and in the middle of this experience, expand your awareness to include your heart, beating right in the middle of your breathing . . .

Quiet Mind Variations

Some of you will find the cognitive-shifting process easy to master. For those who find it somewhat challenging, let me offer you some variations on the basic theme to explore. Hold in mind that the more time and attention you spend right here, mastering this basic shifting process from fixating on a point to seeing everything at once, the deeper all the rest of the coming meditations will move, and the quieter your mind will be throughout.

VARIATION 1: TWO TACTILE SENSATIONS

Because breathing itself can be a great challenge to focus on at first, give the following a try. With your left forefinger, gently rub your left leg with little circles and tune in to the sensation that comes to your mind from this action. At the same time, with your right forefinger, tap your right leg gently. You'll find that when focusing on two tactile sensations at once, and your mind's attention will shift entirely away from your habitual thought flows. Regularly practice this training exercise so that you become intimate with the cognitive-shifting experience.

Feel free to use whatever tactile sensations you want to play with. I find that, wherever I am, I can almost instantly expand my life experience by noticing one obvious sensation (the feel of my left foot touching the ground) and then opening up to notice another sensory input at the same time (my fingers tapping the keyboard). The aim is to regularly quiet the flow of thoughts through the mind so as to enter a quiet experience of the eternal present moment.

Go ahead and try it: move your left forefinger in small circles on your leg . . . and at the same time lightly tap your right forefinger on your right leg . . . focus entirely on the here-and-now expereince . . . enjoy the peace of mind that comes through shifting from past-future cognitive mode into the eternal present of mental quiet.

VARIATION 2: BREATH AND SOUND

Wherever you are and whatever you're doing, you can immediately shift into the meditative mode of quiescence and breath awareness by first becoming aware of the air flowing in and out your nose or mouth and then, at the same time, expanding your awareness to include whatever sounds are coming to your mind. If you listen without being aware of your breathing at the same time, your mind will tend to drift off into associations and thoughts about the sounds coming to you. But by experiencing breath and sound together, your mind lets go of its point fixation and expands. As the mind becomes quiet, you enter into pure experience of the present moment—which is indeed meditation.

Pause and experience your breath sensations . . . and at the same time expand your awareness to include whatever sounds come naturally to you . . .

VARIATION 3: BREATH AND SIGHT

This next variation is found throughout the Buddhist schools of meditation. Be aware of your breathing experience wherever you find it in your body and at the same time expand your awareness to include any object in your visual environment. See the object and be aware of its existence before you and at the same time remain deeply grounded in your own inner breath sensations and experience. Once again, thoughts will naturally disappear in your mind—unless you lose awareness of either the breath or sight experience.

> Look around and find something that you enjoy looking at
> ... while keeping your visual attention focused on this object,
> expand your awareness to include the sensation of the air
> rushing in and out of your nose or mouth ... notice how you
> shift into an expansive, relaxed state of mind, with your
> thoughts quiet ...

VARIATION 4: TWO FEET TOGETHER

Once you start mastering the shift into "wholeness" awareness, you can make the process more subtle by developing the habit of maintaining an ongoing awareness of any two paired body parts, such as both your feet, or both your knees, or both your elbows, or your feet on the ground and your bottom on your seat. By maintaining this expanded awareness as a new positive habit, you'll be able to hold yourself in wholeness consciousness even when you're not meditating—and thus to calm your body, smooth out your emotions, and shift your thoughts into an intuitive-insight mode.

VARIATION 5: LET BACH AND ROCK DO IT

Most of the everyday things that we love to do have the process of "shifting our focus from point to space fixation" built into them.

Making love is surely the most pleasurable example of "two or more sensations at the same time." Music is another beautiful example. One of the reasons we love music so much is that it focuses our attention on the whole. A musical composition can deliver not just one but two or more instruments and melody and harmony lines for our minds to be aware of at the same time. We can stay point-fixated and focus on just one instrument or voice or melody line at a time. But listening to music becomes a transcendent experience when we listen to the bass line and the lead guitar at the same time, or to two or more voices singing harmony, or to the drums and the flute together as a unified sound experience. Bach's treble and bass melody lines naturally challenge us to shift our consciousness into mystic realms in order to hear both of them together, as a whole.

The Silence Beyond

Alan Watts often said in his talks about the spiritual path that "meditation is the act of allowing one's thoughts to cease."

This doesn't mean that all your thoughts cease forever when you meditate. Quieting the mind is not something you once and for all accomplish. Each day you surely spend a lot of time thinking. But each day you can also devote regular periods—sometimes just a few minutes at a time—to entering a state of quiescence where you move beyond thoughts.

In other words, you can strike a healthy balance between thinking and quiescence.

Here's a key point. Inner silence does not block out the sounds of life all around you, nor does it quiet the inner sounds of your heart beating or the air flowing in and out of your body. Quiescence is a quality of consciousness in which your senses come to the fore as your cognition recedes. As you become utterly attentive to all the sounds around you, and through your awareness of these sounds of life, you merge your personal consciousness with the greater consciousness.

Each time you move into a meditative focus, the steady verbal chatter of your thinking mind is replaced by the quiet of your listening mind. You'll reach a point where the natural experience of the volume of your own body and the volume all around you being awakened by your senses, regularly brings you into the mystic reality of the eternal present moment.

Many of us assume that once we quiet our minds, we'll have no more thoughts during meditation. This is not true at all. One of the main reasons for meditating is to learn how to tap your deeper wisdom. When your thinking mind becomes quiet long enough, you can hear what your own heart has to tell you.

Very often, right in the middle of this blessed quiescence, there will emerge a new quality of thought—certain insights, or deep mental reflections of your intuitive, contemplative mind. As you hold your focus on your heart, you'll begin to hear your heart talking and find yourself listening to an inner voice emerging not from your usual thinking center, but rather from some deeper mystic source.

It was surely this inner wisdom that Lao Tzu was talking about when he said,

> Without going out of doors, one can know the world. Without looking through the window, one can realize the Way of Heaven. The farther one goes, the less one knows. Therefore the Sage knows without going out, discriminates without seeing, and accomplishes without action.

Each time we enter into meditation, be it for two minutes or thirty minutes or longer, we're aiming your attention inward toward this deep source of knowing. The intent is to quiet the chronic thoughts that disturb our inner clarity; expand our awareness into a full experience of the vast volume and multiple dimensions of life; and then open up and receive insights and guidance, healing and communion.

Let's end this chapter by moving into a full experience of this process. I'll start this meditation by guiding you through the meditation you learned in the first chapter (breath watch) and then move fairly quickly into our new meditation (quieting the mind). You'll notice that the first and second meditations merge in a seamless flow that naturally quiets your mind. While you focus on your breathing, you'll be led effortlessly into quiescence . . . and contemplation . . . and at some point in your contemplation, into deep meditation . . . and beyond . . .

QUIETING THE MIND: Guided Meditation 2

Allow yourself to relax and get comfortable, preferably sitting upright or perhaps lying on your back . . . and without doing anything at all, just begin to notice how you feel in your body . . . see whether your breathing feels tense or relaxed . . . uneven or smooth . . . give yourself permission to move all you want . . . stretch a few times if that feels good . . . begin to settle into a comfortable balanced position . . .

As you sit comfortably, without judging, just watch the flows of thoughts coming through your mind . . holding your attention a short while . . . then disappearing . . . to be replaced by new thoughts . . . which disappear . . . and are replaced by new thoughts . . . just observe your thoughts coming . . . and going . . .

Let's gently begin to quiet your thought flows . . . turn your attention more and more fully toward your breathing experience here in the present moment . . . feel the actual sensation of the air flowing in . . . and flowing out . . . your nose or mouth as you breathe . . .

Say to yourself, "I am breathing freely" . . . let the inhales and exhales come on their own . . . allow your breathing to stop whenever it wants to, and start again on its own . . . be aware of the air flowing in and out your nose . . . expand your awareness to *also* include the movements in your chest and belly as you breathe . . . *and* also be aware of your heart, beating right in the middle of your breathing . . .

Look to see what emotions you might be feeling in your heart . . . breathe into these feelings . . . accept them . . . let them relax . . . allow your heart to let go of its tensions and aches and pains . . . give yourself permission to just go ahead and feel good, right now . . .

Be aware of your hands . . . your feet . . . your pelvis . . . relax your jaw, your tongue, your face muscles . . . be aware of your whole body, here in this present moment . . .

And how to expand your awareness to include whatever sounds are coming to you . . . just let them come . . . and go . . . and new sounds come . . . and go . . . as you breathe . . . and enjoy the peace of this present moment . . .

Breathing . . . heart . . . whole body . . . sounds . . . the present moment . . . filling you . . . your body relaxed and balanced . . . your breaths coming . . . and going . . .

Say to yourself, "My mind is quiet . . ."

While in this deep peace, reflect upon Lao Tzu's words: "Returning to the root brings quiescence . . ."

And when you're ready, move into deep meditation . . .

FOR INSTANT STREAMED-AUDIO GUIDANCE, PLEASE GO TO
www.7masters.com

CHAPTER 3

Accepting the Truth—Buddha

We've now devoted two chapters to exploring the first two meditations of our *Seven Masters* meditation program. The time we've spent learning to shift our attention devotedly and regularly into the present moment has been time well spent. As most meditation masters have always agreed, "The kingdom of heaven is at hand"—right here and now. Toward this present-moment aim, Buddha taught his universally practiced *Vipassana* meditation, which focuses continually on breath awareness and the quieting of the thoughts flowing through the mind. As Alan Watts says with utmost simplicity in *Still the Mind:*

> When you've found a stable posture, allow your awareness to sink into your breath. . . . You're not trying to cultivate a particular kind of breath. Just gently pay attention to your breathing. Allow the breath to come and go as it may. That's all you need to do. Your body will become still, and your mind will naturally, at some point, become still as well. That is the essential process of meditation.

Life would indeed be wonderful if all we needed to do to attain inner peace and clarity was to follow such brief meditation instruction. If only our thinking minds would surrender easily and regularly be quiet and leave us in peace, we could stop at this point in the book and read no further.

However, even though Buddha and many spiritual teachers before and after him taught that breath awareness is the core spiritual focus, most of them also realized that for most people such utterly simple instruction isn't adequate. Because of our strongly dominant egos, most of us need several additional meditative expansions of consciousness if we're to have a successful spiritual practice.

Solving the Dilemma

The purpose of the third meditation is to encounter directly the busy concerns that won't let you shift into deep meditation. This of course is a skill that takes time to master, so don't be upset if you don't succeed fully the first few times you do this third expansion. After all, we're not judging ourselves based on our superficial success or failure with any of these techniques. In fact, the theme of the third expansion is letting go of all the judgmental thoughts that keep us from accepting the present moment just as it is.

Think on this for a moment: if you could accept yourself right now, and everyone and everything around you, as perfectly okay . . . if you could let go of the idea that there are things in the world and parts of yourself that you just can't accept . . . if you could stop resisting reality and surrender to the present moment as God's perfect creation . . . you'd immediately be able to relax, embrace life, open your heart, and smile at God's creation rather than hold it in judgment.

Aside from physical danger or pain, all that keeps you right now from feeling bright, content, at peace, full of joy, and radiating love is your mind's chronic and often stubborn tendency to refuse to accept reality just as it is in the present moment.

Instead, if you're like almost everyone else, you find yourself possessed by negative beliefs, attitudes, dislikes, desires, and compulsions that keep you locked up in the emotions of anxiety, dissatisfaction, anger, despair, or grief. To see this clearly in one's own life is one of the truly great realizations of the spiritual path.

We're lucky to have Buddha as our primary guide right at this point in our discussion, because two thousand years before modern psychologists started trying to analyze the human psyche, Buddha had already looked inward to his own depths, and realized the basic cause of human unease and suffering—and also the primary path beyond that suffering.

"We are what we think," he stated in the *Dhammapada*. "All that we are arises with our thoughts. . . . How can a troubled mind understand the way? An untroubled mind, no longer seeking to consider what is right and what is wrong, such a mind beyond judgments watches in peace and understands."

Look to Your Heart

In the eyes of Buddha, we learn two things when we master the process of meditation: looking directly at the reality emerging in each present moment; and observing the beliefs and attitudes we carry that fight against that reality by consciously identifying the beliefs and resulting judgments that plague our minds, step by step we can disengage from them so as to attain harmony with reality. In this way, we enter into more and more peace, clarity, and bliss.

Buddha said, "Mistaking the false for the true, you overlook the heart and fill yourself with desire. . . . See the false as false, see the true as true. Look to your heart. Follow your nature."

Like most great spiritual teachers, Buddha often urges us to employ our ability to look, to see, in order to wake up to the truth of the matter. This is the act of meditation. Rather than thinking about reality or being told what is real, we look directly to experience reality, and thus learn what is true for ourselves.

See directly what is true . . . look to your heart . . . follow your nature . . . how are we to do this?

Already in the first and second expansions of our *Seven Masters* meditation you've begun to master the process of shifting your focus from the two-dimensional realm of your thoughts, to the three-dimensional presence of your heart. You're well on your way to being more heartful.

But Buddha realized that most people can't just leap in and succeed by "looking to the heart" without also dealing with the forces of their conditioning that try to pull them away from looking to the heart and knowing the truth.

Therefore, Buddha's formal teaching goes beyond breath meditation, to give us a complete formula and process for dealing with the negative judgments and fears that stand in the way of clear seeing and wakeful living. This liberation process, when approached properly, enables us to look to the very core of our source of suffering, in order to let go of our cherished illusions, and embrace God's creation just the way we find it, in each new moment.

Awakening the Buddha

Who was this man we call the Buddha, and how do his teachings on meditation guide us beyond our own suffering? Siddhartha Gautama was born to wealthy parents in the foothills of the Himalayan Mountains, perhaps a hundred or so years after Lao Tzu disappeared over the pass into historic oblivion in China. (A strong tradition in China and elsewhere maintains that Buddha was the reincarnation of Lao Tzu. Indeed, because their teachings are extremely congruent, Buddhism was able to spread rapidly into China, merging with the Taoist tradition into Chan and then Zen Buddhism.)

Siddhartha lived a life of protected luxury in childhood, married according to his parents' wishes when he was nineteen, and became a father when he was twenty-nine.

Soon thereafter, however, he totally changed his life. Leaving his father's palace, he became a spiritual mendicant, wandering in poverty and fervently seeking liberation from worldly attachments and suffering.

Because he grew up in a traditional Brahmin household, Siddhartha was naturally brought up in the yogic tradition of Hindu teachings, deities, and meditative practice. When he left to explore his own spiritual path, he attempted at first to push those meditative traditions to the extreme in order to attain enlightenment. Finally, after six long years of living in a distant forest disciplining his mind and body to provoke spiritual awakening, but failing to achieve his goal, he gave up traditional approaches to enlightenment and simply struggled to see directly the nature of who he really was at the depths of his spiritual center. Abandoning all goal-orientation in his spiritual quest, he let go of all ego striving and spiritual desires, so that he could finally observe without judgment or attachment, the truth of what he saw and experienced.

While sitting under the famous Boddhi tree at the age of thirty-five, on a cold December morning, he finally realized with a flash of awakening the primal spiritual truths of human existence—and became a Buddha (the term means "awakened one") He returned to his father's palace (his mother had died shortly after his birth) and was recognized even in his hometown as an enlightened teacher. He spent the next forty five years walking from town to town, teaching his path to spiritual awakening.

Today, after more than two thousand years, that path is still a primary spiritual process taught throughout the world. And the core realization of that path, in the utterly simple and complete words of the Buddha: "How wonderful, how wonderful! All things are perfect, exactly as they are!"

In other words, right now, without the need to change anything at all, without the requirement to do anything, we live in a perfect universe. There is nothing we need to change in order to be perfect and enlightened. All we need to do is realize in meditation that beyond all our judgments and worries, goals and expectations, the perfection of awakening and fulfillment exists within us already, right now, in this eternal moment.

Again in Buddha's words: "With single-mindedness, the master quells his thoughts. He ends their wandering. Seated in the cave of the heart, he finds freedom."

The mystic realization of Buddha—and countless other awakened beings over the ages—has been that God's creation is indeed perfect in every way. Regardless of how we judge it from our own point of view, with all our prejudices and expectations, the present moment is utterly perfect.

Ah, but how our minds resist accepting this truthful spiritual observation! Our thinking minds are so full of beliefs about how things "should be" rather than how things "are" that we refuse to accept reality as it is. We insist that our inner dreams and expectations must become fulfilled in order for us to accept things. And so we confuse and distort and reject and deny the simple reality of the present moment, because that reality doesn't match our ego's image of how the world should be. Thus arises suffering—from our ignorance of the truth of life and our refusal to accept that truth. Our own minds separate us from our own deeper nature, our Buddhahood.

How can we break beyond the ignorance and prejudice, the fears and denials of our attitudes and judgments, so that we see clearly the truth of the perfection of life and enter into our own Buddha nature?

Facts of Life

Along with being a fully awakened being spiritually, Buddha was perhaps the greatest psychologist of all time. Indeed, his primary claim to fame is that he observed the functioning of the human mind (his own) and saw to the utter depths how it works in its usual conditioned and mostly unconscious mode—and how it can be trained and guided toward a psychological and spiritual awakening that reveals the mind's true nature to itself.

In his Four Noble Truths, or primary facts of life, Buddha taught the following:

First Noble Truth: An unawakened human being regularly suffers through all of life's hardships, pains, heartbreaks, hungers, desires, disillusionments, and failings. In our un-awakened state, we cannot avoid life's sufferings—they're part of the human cognitive dilemma. Especially because of our judgmental thoughts and emotions, we tend to live in a tor-ture chamber of our own creation.

Second Noble Truth: The primary cause of our suffering is not our present-moment experience, but rather our response to it, what we think about it, and all the mental activity we create surrounding our present situation. In other words, the moment-to-moment physical pain in life is minor in compari-son to the emotional and psychic suffering that we habitually inflict on ourselves, through all our chronic thoughts, beliefs, expectations, desires, and denials concerning the reality of life. We think thoughts that make us unhappy with our situation and lead us to crave a different reality than the one we're in—and this craving generates our unhappiness. We want to change what we don't like in life, and everything we like and are attached to we want to go on forever—even though reality dictates differently. Thus, in Buddhist teachings, all our suffer-ing is an expression and a reflection of the distance between reality and our desires and beliefs.

Third Noble Truth: There exists an expanded state of mind in which we wake up to our greater nature beyond our ego minds and all the suffering generated by our thoughts and cravings. We need not remain limited to our programmed beliefs, cultural assumptions, and animal instincts. We carry within, our own Buddha nature—in which we are alive in the present moment in total acceptance of reality and therefore free of the habitual tortures of our thinking and judging minds.

Fourth Noble Truth: There is a logical, specific meditative path we can learn to walk that frees us from the habitual dissatisfaction of conditioned existence, and liberates us from chronic fear and craving. We can act right now on our own, just as Buddha did, to encourage an awakened spiritual state called *nirvana*, or *satori*, or Buddhahood. In this process we choose to let go of our ego identity and our fears of surrender, thus allowing ourselves to be born again into a new state of consciousness—in which we realize our perfect nature, perceive reality directly and truthfully, and are no longer prisoners of our own mental beliefs and cravings.

Facing Reality Unafraid

Buddha taught that "the one who has conquered himself is a far greater hero than he who has defeated a thousand times a thousand men." But wait—if we're already perfect, what is there to conquer? Aren't we supposed to just sit quietly and make no effort as we realize who we really are? What's all this aggressive talk about conquering our own selves?

If you've been sitting and turning your attention to your breathing and looking inward to your own deeper identity, you already know the answer to this question. Who or what is it, after all, that continually pulls your attention away from the simple act of looking to your center to see who you really are? Obviously there is a battle going on—some mental power is resisting the simple spiritual act of shining the light of consciousness toward your ultimate inner source.

Buddha recognized this ego presence that feels threatened by and therefore fears the truth. He observed, as we all have, that some part of us is afraid to face reality head-on. The simple fact is that our ego, our concept of who we are, has been constructed since early childhood out of beliefs and desires, parental assumptions and cultural conditionings, that are not necessarily a true reflection of reality.

When we deeply contemplate our own nature, as we do in this third meditation, we inevitably begin to realize that the "I" we identify with is nothing more than a construct of our own phenomenally clever minds. We have created a vast mental concept of who we are, and it is almost never a clear reflection of reality. To see reality clearly, we must learn to let go of all our cherished beliefs about who we are and what life in general is all about.

I have found repeatedly throughout the spiritual literature of all meditative teachings, one particular lesson that my grandfather taught me: that we can't hold one thing tightly in our grasp, and at the same time reach out and take something new. We must let go of and put aside what we are grasping, in order to be able to receive something that we want or need much more.

All spiritual and psychological growth requires a letting go of a limited belief in order to open up and receive a more expansive belief—or even better, a direct experience of reality that makes all beliefs unnecessary.

This is the challenge of spiritual growth: to enlighten the ego to where it realizes, through more and more meditative experience, that letting go of judgments about reality and embracing reality itself, is not only worthwhile but essential to a truly fulfilling life.

The primary problem with such liberation that Buddha observed, was that the ego is fearful of its own demise—and will fight hard to preserve its limited and often unrealistic grounding. The ego must be properly related with and instructed in meditation to where it sees that by preserving the illusory myth of its own existence, it is resisting its own expansion and revelation.

The challenge that Buddha offers our ego presence is to learn how to conquer the fears within us that run away from the light, that resist change, that can't face the obliteration of our illusions in the act of entering the light.

Lama Surya Das puts it this way in his book *Awakening the Buddha Within:*

> As you walk the inner path of awakening, recognize that it is most definitely a heroic journey. You must be prepared to make sacrifices, and yes, you must be prepared to change. Just as a caterpillar must shed its familiar cocoon in order to become a butterfly and fly, you must be willing to change and shed the hard armor of self-centered egotism. As compelling as the inner journey is, it can be difficult because it brings you face to face with reality. It brings you face to face with who you really are.

As Buddha teaches, even when we're devoted to walking the spiritual path, our ingrained psychological constructs and habits tend to negatively distance us from our true spiritual nature and thus generate chronic feelings of confusion, angst, and suffering. Human beings avoid waking up to their true nature for only one reason—their ego identity is afraid to give up control and surrender to a reality that's overwhelmingly greater than the ego's concept of reality.

The following meditations are designed to meet your ego right where it presently finds itself in the transformation process. They provide a safe process through which fears can be steadily put aside and reality explored in more and more depth, with each new meditation session. Step by gentle step, your beliefs and cherished assumptions, your apprehensions and even your resolute stubbornness in the face of change, can pause and experience the touch of truth, the strength of reality, the loving power of your own spiritual core . . . and thus willingly begin to let go the old, in order to embrace the new.

Who are you really when you look inside? Is your identity nothing more than a figment of your own imagination and past experience, or a consciousness and presence that exist beyond your ego construct?

When you think of who you are as a personality, as an ego identity, is there anything there at all, beyond the images and memories and myths and beliefs about who you are, that you've created over the years, and that other people's images of you have created?

Pause and Reflect

After reading this paragraph, you might want to put the book aside and tune in to your breathing . . . your heart . . . your whole body here in this present moment . . . allow your mind to become quiet . . . and in this quiet reflective state, say to yourself, "I am (your name)," and then ask yourself: Who is this person really? Look to see the truth . . .

Love or Judgment

There are two primary pillars to the Buddhist understanding of the spiritual path. One is the challenge of opening our personal awareness to the reality of life and developing our sense of wisdom and perspective regarding who we are and what life is all about. This is primarily a function of the mind.

The other great pillar is the challenge of developing our ability to feel compassion and acceptance toward all of God's creation. This is primarily a function of the heart.

Compassion is a quality that we discover only when we begin to stop judging the world, and begin loving it. This third meditation, about accepting reality just as it is, naturally leads us into an exploration of our capacity to feel love in our hearts and ultimately to love unconditionally, as Buddha and Jesus and most other spiritual masters encourage us to do.

The simple fact is this: we cannot judge something, and feel love for it, at the same time. Why? Because the very process of judgment is rooted in a part of our brain, the amygdala, that is fear-based. This red-alert area, directly linked to our senses and our cognitive functions, tells us to determine first whether anything in our immediate environment is a threat to us. All animals have this fear-based survival mechanism of judgment, and certainly it's essential for physical survival.

Our human dilemma is that not only do we observe the present moment to see whether there's any danger, but we also have the capacity to remember bad things that happened to us in the past and to imagine these things happening to us in the future. This is what worrying is all about.

Ultimately most human suffering comes from our propensity to imagine possible scenarios in the future and either become anxious over a negative scenario, or overly eager to fulfill a positive scenario. In either case, our imaginings about the future tend to create suffering in the present moment.

If you contemplate the suffering that happens to you day in and day out, you'll quickly notice that a lot of suffering is emotional and mental rather than physical. And even with physical pain, we tend to amplify the actual pain with all sorts of worries that make us suffer far beyond the effects of our physical condition.

Buddha saw all this clearly. The Four Noble Truths clarified what psychologists are just now coming to understand as the root cause of human suffering—our mental fixation on fear-based beliefs, apprehensions, and imaginations. Upon careful examination, we find that our desire to escape suffering is directly responsible for most of our cravings and desires as well. Only when we're suffering do we have the reflex to try to do something that will make us feel better.

When we take away the underlying fear, we eliminate the craving. And when we eliminate the craving to change our situation, we find our minds becoming quiet, our perception clearing, our hearts opening . . . and our spirits soaring.

Our challenge is to regularly pause in meditation, tune in to our breathing . . . our heart . . . our presence right here and now . . . and without judging what we find, observe ourselves in the present moment, noticing the emotions we are feeling and the thoughts, attitudes, and beliefs that are generating those feelings. We can then see clearly that those attitudes and beliefs are causing us to suffer. When we see this clearly, we can begin to let go of such attitudes.

This is the healing process, and as Buddha emphasized repeatedly, all it requires is a direct looking and an honest seeing and accepting of what we find. This seeing in itself generates the transformation. It enables us to accept reality just as it is, because it's entirely foolish to fight reality.

In this acceptance we find that we can open our hearts to the world around us, and allow compassion to flow . . .

The Ultimate Fear

When you come to this third expansion in your meditations, I encourage you regularly to pause and enter into deep contemplation upon the nature of fear itself. Become a serious student of fear. Look it right in the eye. Read everything you can find on it.

Right here and now in this meditative context, I am challenging and encouraging you over and over, to look directly inward without judgment at all your worries and anxious mental habits. Catch them in the act of muddying the spiritual waters and causing you chronic emotional anguish. And as Krishnamurti and Buddha assert, in that act of seeing with great immediacy how your fearful thoughts generate suffering inside you and distance you from your own heart, you'll suddenly realize that you are torturing yourself with illusory worries—and awaken to the fact that you yourself are not those fears at all.

I challenge you to find a single fear that runs through your mind that is not rooted in your fear of your own demise. Our entire fear mechanism is grounded in doing its best to keep us alive as long as possible. Every small danger we encounter pushes the fear button that makes us feel the unavoidable presence of our own coming death.

This is why a central teaching of all spiritual traditions is that to overcome fear we must face our own mortality, look deeper into what life is all about, and ultimately discover our spiritual core of being that is not identified with this particular body and this particular brain and this particular ego dream.

All mystic experience is grounded in the direct perception and knowing that our individual consciousness is not in any way separate from the greater consciousness. We saw how Lao Tzu began the *Tao Te Ching* by talking about the One, the Infinite, the Unified Reality of which we are integral parts. Buddha spoke the same way—our true identity is always as the infinite eternal Buddha. Jesus likewise taught of being one with God and having eternal life. Mohammed the same.

There is no past or future beyond the constructs of our imagining minds. In meditation we escape the suffering caused by fear of death and all the rest, by holding our focus of attention devotedly to this present moment, trusting utterly in our perception that this present moment is perfect. Even if the bombs are falling on our heads, the present moment is perfect. Why? Because whatever happens to us, if we don't go into fear, we remain eternally in God's perfect creation.

Pause and Experience

Pause for a few moments now and just watch your breathing . . . observe whether you feel any anxiety or worry or apprehension in your body . . . look to see what thoughts or imaginations are generating your feelings . . . notice what happens when you begin to quiet those thoughts . . .

Judge Not

Whenever we express an opinion about something, we're judging based on our beliefs and prejudices. Whenever a thought labels something one way or another, we've judged based on our ego's personal evaluation system. Whenever we decide to act in a particular way based on what we think is right and wrong, we've judged the situation. Each time we react with the feeling of anger, apprehension, repulsion, or avoidance, we've reacted with a judgment of the situation. Even when we decide that it's a beautiful day, that we really like potato salad, that taking a trip to Siam would be a great way to spend the vacation, we've experienced the judgmental function of our mind.

- How much of your waking day is filled with judgmental thoughts?

- To what extent are your thoughts distancing you from your own Buddha nature?

- To what extent are your thoughts fear-based and therefore making you suffer?

- What would your life be like if you stopped judging everything and everyone around you and accepted them just as they are?

During the next days and weeks I suggest that you develop the discipline of watching your own flow of thoughts as much as possible to see how often you're in judgment mode. The very act of seeing your mental habits that cause you suffering will stimulate a movement beyond such mental habits. The seeing is in itself the response. That's a primary dynamic of the power of meditation.

Direct Impact

Probably at least half the population of this world has heard the powerful psychological and spiritual principle as articulated by Jesus: "Don't judge, or you will be judged yourself; because with the judgment you use to judge the world, you yourself will be judged."

The first two words of this saying can hit like a massive jolt to our system. One of the world's most remarkable spiritual teachers is telling us that it's not a good idea to be in judgment mode at all, and yet we know we go around judging almost constantly, both negatively and positively. Buddha made the same observation over and over in his teachings. Being locked into the ego's judgment games is not productive spiritually, and it generates suffering.

It's important to remember that when we look at a rose and go through the mental process of judging the rose as beautiful and say to ourselves, "Oh, what a marvelous rose!" we are standing in judgment of that rose, even if it's a positive judgment. And in the very process of spending time evaluating and then thinking our positive-judgment thoughts, we temporarily distance ourselves from the direct impact of the rose.

We can't experience reality and also judge it at the same time. Psychologically, judgment is a comparative function of the mind in which we evaluate present perceptual inputs by comparing them with past perceptual inputs. This mental process moves us away from the present moment . . . we're lost in thought while we're judging. Therefore, any spiritual teacher who values full participation in the present moment will agree with Jesus and Buddha and recommend that we function in judgment mode as little as possible, so as to be fully engaged with the world rather than lost in thought.

Pause and Experience

After reading this paragraph, put the book aside . . . sit comfortably . . . and tune in to your breathing experience. First just observe your breathing . . . then look around at the world that surrounds you . . . observe whether your mind is quiet or whether thoughts begin to flow . . . notice whether these are creative thoughts or judgmental thoughts . . . are you accepting the world just as it is, or are you somehow not satisfied with the world around you? . . .

Accepting the World

In this third meditative expansion we're relying a great deal on the contemplative function of the mind, in looking to see right to the heart of our beliefs and habits and how they influence our emotions and spiritual experience.

Our theme for this chapter is "I accept the world just as it is." From the point of view of deep contemplation, what does it really mean to accept the world just as it is? This question will be your starting point each time you come to this third expansion, to help you look more deeply into all the issues we've been discussing.

For instance, take time to look deeply into the nature of acceptance. Set aside entire meditation sessions to tune in to your breathing . . . your heart . . . your whole body here in this present moment . . . allow your mind to become quiet . . . and in this quiet state of mind, begin to allow your mind to contemplate the quality of acceptance . . .

If you say the focus phrase "I accept the world just as it is" and feel tense in your breathing and heart, look to see what thoughts are running through your mind that make you say, "Heck no, I don't accept the world out there, because . . ." Take a look at those thoughts, those judgments that are polluting your mind and soul. And go a step further to look at the fear that underlies the judgment.

Often we find that some image from the evening news, from a conversation, from something we read or saw that day, is still sticking in our craw, generating worried or angry thoughts and imaginings just below the surface of our conscious mind. Meditation is a wonderful tool for catching subconscious thoughts that are causing tensions and fears and aggressive feelings.

Once you pause and catch those thoughts, you can call their bluff by evaluating the judgment and the worry, and asking yourself honestly whether there's any point in holding on to them.

Ask yourself, what is the core dilemma that seems to be threatening me? Am I really threatened? If my well-being is indeed threatened, then perhaps it's wise to think logically about the situation and plan a course of action to resolve the danger. Otherwise, even the logic of the thinking mind will realize that it's foolish to be tense and upset in the present moment, when there is no present-moment danger.

With this realization that there is no present-moment danger surrounding me, I'm usually able to relax and, indeed, accept the world just as it is, at least for the next ten or twenty minutes of meditation. Sometimes I allow this third meditation to fill my entire meditation time, if this feels good and natural. Sometimes, however, even if I find that I can't quite accept the world just as it is right at that moment, I go ahead and move on to the fourth meditation—because the resolution of my feelings of not accepting the world is often to be found in the fourth meditation, or the fifth.

So be sure not to get stuck in one of the early expansions. Even if your breathing remains tense, even if your mind doesn't get quiet right away, even if you can't accept the world just as it is, just continue moving through the expansions. At some point, almost always, the tensions will clear and the present moment will open up in all its meditative perfection. This meditation program is designed to allow you great freedom to expand at whatever pace seems natural for you at the moment.

Sometimes you'll naturally move through all seven meditations quite quickly, saying each focus phase and experiencing its impact on your consciousness, then moving on to the next meditation phrase, and the next, so that in just a few minutes you cover all seven bases, and then move into deep unstructured meditation.

At other times you'll get perhaps as far the third meditation and find that you want to spend time contemplating your present fears and judgments, as you look deeply for five to ten minutes in the direction the focus phrase points you.

Contemplating Acceptance

Whenever you find yourself wanting to enter into deep contemplation on the theme of "I accept the world just as it is," you might want to ask yourself these questions:

- Many people fear that if they accept everything the way it is, they'll be stuck with things just as they are forever. Is this true?

- Do we bring about positive change through judging the present situation negatively and using manipulation to change things, or through accepting the reality of the present situation and agreeing to participate in a spirit of unconditional love and compassion?

- When we deny reality, is anything positive ever accomplished?

- Is there an inherent danger in refusing to accept reality?

- Is it possible to be judging and feel love at the same time?

- Are you your own harshest critic? Is your self-judgment valid or is it based on questionable assumptions and beliefs?

- Who are you when you accept yourself unconditionally?

Pause and Reflect

Pause if you'd like . . . take time to tune in to your breathing, your whole-body presence in the here and now . . . and go through this list of questions again, allowing yourself to move deeply into contemplation . . .

Surrendering

W hen we do not accept the world just as it is, we are assuming that the world is not to be trusted and that the universe is not unfolding as it should. Your ego mind carries a great array of beliefs about how the world should be. Even if your belief is positive and deeply spiritual, you must still face the fact that if your belief about how the world should be does not match the reality of how the world is, you are generating suffering inside yourself, and thus conflict, by holding on to a belief that doesn't match reality.

In her book *Loving What Is,* Byron Katie hits this psychological nail on the head:

> If you want reality to be different than it is, you might as well try to teach a cat to bark. You can try and try, and in the end the cat will look up at you and say, "Meow." Wanting reality to be different than it is, is hopeless. . . . We can know that reality is good just as it is, because when we argue with it, we experience tension and frustration. We don't feel natural and balanced. When we stop opposing reality, action becomes simple, fluid, kind, and fearless.

There it is—when we stop opposing reality and accept the world just as it is, we become loving and fearless. And when that fear is gone, our cravings disappear and we're effortlessly able to open our hearts to full participation in the eternal present moment.

I want to suggest that you explore fully what it means to surrender to reality. And then, just give up fighting reality. Don't spend another second wishing reality were different. Right now, right in this moment, it is imperative to accept reality because there is nothing you can do to change the present moment. This is the spiritual understanding of life. The present moment is perfect—simply because it can be no other way. This is it.

The magical logic is that only by fully surrendering to the present moment can we gain the power to participate in its unfolding, and have a positive impact on coming moments. By living fully in the here and now with zero resistance to what is, we become full participants in the present moment. And through this surrender and acceptance and participation, we bring the power of love and spiritual truth to the present moment—and all our actions become natural, in harmony and resonant with spiritual truth. Our reality and the reality of the world around us come into synch.

Only when this happens do we make genuinely positive progress—not through the manipulation of our judging minds, but through the participation of our spiritual souls. By surrendering to reality, we very clearly surrender to God and allow Spirit to act through us, rather than allowing our fearful ego to determine our actions. Thus do we learn to bring the meditative quality of mind and soul into action in the world.

ACCEPTING THE TRUTH: Guided Meditation 3

> Make sure you're comfortable and sitting however you choose . . . make whatever movements you want to . . . and gently turn your attention to the air flowing in and out of your nose or mouth . . . expand your awareness to include the movements in your chest and belly as you breathe . . . say to yourself, "I'm breathing freely . . ."
>
> At the same time, be aware of your heart, right in the middle of your breathing . . . be aware of your whole body, here in

this present moment . . . your feet . . . your hands . . . your face . . . your whole being . . . be aware of the sounds around you . . . and say to yourself, "My mind is quiet . . ."

Expand your awareness to include the world around you . . . the room you're in . . . the building you're in . . . the people in your family . . . in your community . . . the people you work with . . . the people driving the highways . . . everyone and everything they're doing right now . . . the world just as it is in this moment . . . God's perfect creation . . . and say to yourself, "I accept the world just as it is . . ."

Notice your breathing . . . how you feel in your heart . . . observe whatever thoughts might be flowing through your mind about accepting or judging the world around you . . . *notice if* there's something that someone has done, or should have done, or shouldn't have done, that upsets you or makes you angry . . . be aware of any physical tension or emotional suffering that *might be inside you,* being provoked by something in the world that you don't like . . . that you reject . . . that makes you angry . . . or afraid . . . is there anything or anyone in the world that you're not accepting right now in this moment?

Notice that right now, right here, you're not being threatened *in this moment* . . . you're safe, you're secure, you're entirely okay right now . . . so just for the next few breaths, see *if* you can go ahead and let go of all your judgments and worries, concerns and apprehensions, dislikes and condemnations . . . and just relax pleasurably into the experience of releasing your worries and judgments, and accepting the world right now just as it is . . .

Observe *what changes might* come over you emotionally, in your heart especially, when you say to yourself a few times, "I accept the world just as it is . . ."

If you want, begin to imagine that you're in a room at a table with two chairs . . . you're relaxed, and not feeling threatened or upset at all . . . you're at peace inside, and at peace with the world around you . . . someone you've had conflict with walks into the room . . . look and see who it is . . . this person comes over to the table and sits down across from you . . . rather than judging this person, rather than reacting with anger or rejection or apprehension, just stay with your breathing . . . remain calm and feeling good in your body . . . hold your focus in your heart region . . . you can look this person gently, nonjudgmentally in the eye . . . and without any fear at all, experience opening your heart to this person . . . see this person in all his or her own suffering, as part of God's perfect creation . . . allow a smile of compassion and acceptance to touch your expression as you say, "I accept you just as you are."

Observe how it feels to let go of judging and to accept. Notice how the other person responds when he or she no longer feels judged by you . . . if you feel so moved, you can stand up, walk over to the person, and give him or her a hug . . . as this person leaves the room, notice how you feel in your heart.

And now, let go of the imagined scene . . . tune in to your breathing . . . your heart . . . your whole body here in this present moment, and say again to yourself, "I accept the world just as it is . . ."

Allow a beautiful feeling of acceptance to fill you . . . loving reality just as it is . . . you can't change the reality of the moment . . . you can only embrace God's creation . . . and enjoy being alive right now . . . surrendering to what is . . . breathing . . . your awareness expanding . . . no resistance . . . here and now . . . breathing . . . enjoying life . . . and expanding into a new experience . . .

FOR INSTANT STREAMED-AUDIO GUIDANCE, PLEASE GO TO
www.7masters.com

CHAPTER 4

Heart Awakening—Jesus

This crucial chapter lies directly in the middle of our seven meditations because, in many ways, we have arrived at the heart of our meditation program. Not only Jesus but Buddha, Lao Tzu, and Patanjali before him, and Mohammed, Gurdjieff, and Krishnamurti after him, all considered the heart and its primal capacity to receive and share universal unconditional love and wisdom to be the epicenter of spiritual life.

In this chapter, we call primarily on the teachings, inspiration, and enduring spiritual presence of Jesus of Nazareth, who lived at the beginning of our calendar of years. A great many people call him the Christ, and many others consider him one of the truly awakened beings ever to walk this earth. Whether you consider yourself a practicing Christian or not, I hope you'll find the insights we gain in this chapter of special value.

The fourth and fifth expansions of our *Seven Masters* meditation program will help you reawaken your relationship with your own heart, and the love that flows into that spiritual center. Most of us tend to have considerable difficulty with our heart feelings and insights. For various reasons we'll explore shortly, we're afraid to focus on our heart's presence—and instead tend to stay focused in our minds. Jesus, Buddha, and Lao Tzu all specifically challenge us to let go of such mental fixations, and surrender to the wisdom of our hearts.

Pause and Reflect

How does this general notion of heart-focused living strike you? Pause for a few moments after reading this paragraph, put the book aside . . . and ask yourself, where do you most enjoy having your focus of attention in your body? . . . up in your head and brain region or deep in your chest and heart region? . . . contemplate a moment on your relationship with your own heart . . . look directly and see what you discover in this new moment . . .

Looking for Jesus

I arrived in San Francisco in the summer of 1968 to attend the Presbyterian-run San Francisco Theological Seminary, which was attached to UC Berkeley's Graduate Theological Union. For the next five years, while getting degrees in pastoral psychology and comparative religions, I did my best to fit into the Protestant approach to spiritual life while also becoming involved in Kriya yoga, Sufi dancing, and the wild, inspiring Zen world of Alan Watts.

San Francisco Theological Seminary was perhaps the most exciting seminary to be found in America theologically, but to my dismay, the more I looked for a meditative dimension to the Protestant tradition, the more frustrated I became. There was simply no contemplative tradition to be found in formal Protestant life, and most professors had no interest in discussing the spiritual value of a meditative practice.

My key insights into the Christian understanding of meditation came from an entirely unexpected source—a mystery man who seemed to appear out of nowhere and quickly became a central figure in the San Francisco meditation world. This man was around twenty-five, obviously Asian, with long black hair and a tall slender body. When he first appeared, he was wearing a simple dark red robe—this was the early seventies when people wore whatever they wanted to in San Francisco. He had a deep but quiet voice and spoke fluent English with a hard-to-pinpoint accent.

Although he apparently had absolutely no money, within a week of his appearance he was living in a large house someone had lent him in Berkeley, and teaching fifty people a special meditation program he said he'd learned from his own teacher in Southeast Asia.

He told us very little about his past except that he had been orphaned at age five, then adopted by a Christian missionary couple and raised in their mission. When he was twelve, his adoptive parents left their missionary work and moved with him to study in the mountains with a Buddhist master, whose name he never mentioned.

Key to the theme of this chapter and meditation was the single visit that this young man made to my seminary one afternoon. Right after an afternoon lecture in the main lecture hall, there he was, standing quietly in the back, dressed in Levis, sneakers, and T-shirt, as was now his preference. The teacher waved for him to come forward.

For the next half-hour in front of this group of Christian students, he talked quietly of having first learned about the love that Jesus brought into the world from his adopted missionary parents, who radiated a special quality of acceptance and compassion everywhere they went. He then talked about a simple yet penetrating mystic experience he had while looking through the Bible one morning as a child. He discovered as he flipped somewhat randomly through the pages that certain passages in the Bible seemed to grab his attention, even to radiate light when he read them.

He turned and wrote on the blackboard the following six fragments of quotes from the Bible:

God is love

Fear not

Be still

Know the truth

Love your neighbor as you love yourself

Love one another as I have loved you

As he put down the chalk he said softly, "I have found that if I meditate upon these words, and live them, there is nothing missing. This is the spiritual path as taught in your tradition. You need nothing more to bring the Holy Spirit into your lives, and when you have the Spirit, you can put all else aside. Love is all there is. Let's live it."

With his characteristic humble shrug, he smiled warmly, then turned and walked down the aisle and out of the room. For another month or so he guided students through much the same meditations that I'm teaching you in this book. He regularly taught us how to hold our mind's attention on our heart region . . . to forgive one another, and accept reality as it is . . . to listen quietly to God speaking through our hearts . . . and to allow love to flow into our hearts and out into the world.

I felt I'd finally found my true spiritual teacher in this mysterious young man, who fully lived what he taught and integrated the world meditation teachings into a cohesive whole that I could readily experience in my own heart. Then one afternoon he calmly approached us, wearing his old robe. He smiled softly, shook hands, said good-bye . . . and walked out the door, never to be seen again.

Pause and Experience

You might want to pause after reading this paragraph, close your eyes, and tune in to your breathing . . . your heart . . . and begin to open your heart to the presence of these special teachers who come to us when we need them, either in person or in spirit . . . Does your heart feel open to ask for, and receive, spiritual guidance? See what insights come to you . . .

God Is Love

Einstein reduced the nature of the entire universe to one simple equation that we all know by heart if not by scientific understanding: $E = MC^2$. The Judeo-Christian tradition reduced the entire spiritual reality of human existence to another, even more succinct equation: God = Love. This ultimate truth stands as the foundation of Jesus' teachings and in actual practice is such a radical notion that our thinking minds simply cannot grasp it.

Why is this? Because love is not a concept. It is not an idea. It is not a belief. It is the positive life force and integrating power that creates and holds all reality together.

In the same way that the ancient Taoists and Hebrews insisted that we cannot adequately conceptualize and thus name and categorize the ultimate presence and being that created our physical universe, we cannot conceptualize and name the underlying power that sustains life in this universe. Yes, it is true that, from a spiritual point of view, we call that underlying power "love." But this term only points in the direction of that creative sustaining force—it cannot fully capture the force conceptually. Science studies the manifest physical reality of the universe. Love is the infinite creative force that continually manifests physical reality.

The Taoists understood this situation quite clearly: "The name that can be named is not the Eternal Name. The Unnameable is originator of Heaven and Earth. Mystery of mysteries—that is the gate of all wonderful essence."

And how do we pass through that gate? Jesus said, "Ask, and it will be given to you; seek it, and you'll find it. Knock, and the door will open." Wherever and whenever one or more people pause and tune in to their hearts and open up to love, it comes flowing into their hearts. That's the perennial truth that all human beings live by spiritually. God is love, and we can readily encounter and commune with God by opening our hearts to love.

Just as Lao Tzu, Patanjali, and Buddha were ultimate expressions of a long and fruitful spiritual tradition before them, likewise Jesus emerged from a tradition that had been evolving in its relationship with the divine for thousands of years. In the Old Testament, the book of Exodus proclaims that "God is compassionate and gracious, and abounding in loving kindness and truth." In Psalm 36 the Psalmist sings, "How precious is Your loving kindness, God!"

In early times the gods whom people worshiped were very often feared because they were anything but loving gods. The great leap forward that Judaism represented in world religious evolution was that tradition's realization that the one God who is the creator and sustainer of all reality is loving and compassionate, full of forgiveness and support.

Buddha likewise taught that compassion is central to meditation. The difference in this regard between Buddhism and Taoism, on the one hand, and Christianity and Islam on the other, is that the latter focus on a very personal God, whereas Buddhism and Taoism are not theist traditions. When we let go of our religious

beliefs on the matter, we each come to discover, through meditation, our individual preference for a more personal sense of God,
or the direct encounter with Spirit without any personal deity. I
myself find that some days in meditation I feel the presence of a
personal deity very strongly, but often the experience is of pure
oneness with the Tao with no personal overtones.

Please give yourself the freedom to open up and discover your
own evolving relationship with the divine. God is love, yet our experience of that love comes in many different forms and qualities.
As we contemplate the actual experience of love flowing into our
hearts, and our response to this inflow, most of us realize that we
usually block this flow and feel shut off from the presence of the
Tao in our lives. We cannot feel the touch of God's hand on our
hearts. The aim in this meditation program is not to explore theo-
retically the idea of such love, or to create a romantic vision of
being loving, but to learn the pragmatic steps involved in opening
our hearts to love more deeply.

Three of the short biblical teachings I listed earlier have been
my own guiding lights in exploring the psychological and spiritual
path to transcending emotional contractions and letting the love
flow. My meditations on these three teachings indicate that the act
of letting go of fear, quieting the mind, and opening up to experience the truth, regardless of what it might be, leads directly to
heart awakening.

Let's look at each of these teachings in turn to see how they can
become a lifetime meditative practice.

Fear Not

As we've already explored in chapter 3, fear is the great killer
of spiritual experience. When we're caught up in worries, apprehensions, dreads, and anxieties, psychologically we lose our
ability to feel empathy for others—and indeed, for our own selves.
By extension, we lose our ability to relate in love with our deeper

spiritual core of being. In other words, we lose touch with God when we're afraid.

There are sixty-two places in the Bible where God or Jesus says: "Fear not." Genesis, the first book of the Bible, tells us: "The word of God came to Abram in a vision, saying, fear not." And just a short time later, "God appeared to him and said . . . fear not, for I am with you." Jesus associated the letting go of fear with healing: "Jesus came and touched them and he said, 'Stand up, and do not be afraid.'" To those who were worried about the terrible things that might happen in the future, Jesus said: "You will hear about wars. You will hear that war is coming. But do not be caught up in fear."

And perhaps most important to our understanding of fear are Jesus' memorable words: "Peace is what I leave for you. I give you my own peace. Do not let anything trouble your hearts. Do not fear."

This is so clear—don't let anything trouble your hearts. Don't be afraid of anything. Live outside the grip of debilitating anxieties and apprehensions.

But how?

As a therapist, I've found only one way to move beyond the grip of fear—to walk the meditative path, to learn to quiet the mind and let go of the thought flows that generate our worries and anxieties, to open our hearts to be filled with fear's opposite—love.

Cognitive psychology has demonstrated scientifically during the last thirty years that anxiety is not a free-standing emotion, nor are chronic forebodings and apprehensions independent moods. Rather, they emerge directly from the habitual negative thoughts and imaginings that run through our minds. The primary psychological fact is that unless we're being directly threatened physically, it always takes a thought to make us feel anxious.

Clearly, we can act on this research insight and remove fear from our lives by learning to distance ourselves from those thoughts that generate the emotional and physiological reactions of fear. This is exactly what we do in this approach to meditation.

We learn to "be still" and, in so doing, gain access to that special quality of spiritual peace that Jesus spoke about so often.

You'll note that in the first three chapters we focused concertedly on mastering meditation techniques that enable us to quiet the flow of thoughts through our minds. Jesus gave the clear spiritual order: stop living in fear. Let's take the challenge—our spiritual lives depend on it.

I've found over the years that psychological treatment of anxiety without a spiritual meditative dimension almost always fails. Cognitive therapy can fill our heads with positive thoughts that block out the negative thoughts, but only when we learn to quiet all thoughts entirely do we really enter into the "peace that passes all understanding," as the Psalmist put it. I've also learned that eliminating fear-based thoughts and images and becoming receptive to the inflow of spiritual love is an act of will—that we must consciously choose love, over fear over and over again until it becomes our new modus operandi.

Pause and Reflect

Is anxiety a major issue in your life? Do you find that worries tend to cloud your mind and close your heart? Feel free to pause a few moments here, put the book aside, tune in to your breathing . . . and reflect on the primary need to let your worries go if you want to fill your heart with love.

Be Still, and Know

Stillness is the essence of meditation, and the antithesis of a fearful state. We cannot relax and be at peace in our hearts, we cannot open to the inflow of love, when our minds are disturbed and not at rest. Deep within the Judeo-Christian tradition we find clear expression of the value and necessity of stillness. In Psalm 4 we are told to "commune with your own heart upon your bed, and be still." And in Psalm 46 comes the most powerful instruction: "Be still, and know that I am God."

In Psalm 107 we are told that "they were glad because they were quiet, so God guided them to their desired haven." In Isaiah we are instructed: "In repentance and rest you will be saved, in quietness and trust is your strength. . . . How long will you not be quiet? Withdraw . . . be at rest, and stay still." There it is—the meditative tradition that nurtured Jesus in his childhood and surely through his spiritual awakening.

In the midst of this meditative quietness we begin to see directly into the truth of life, and fulfill what Jesus taught with his most powerful meditative imperative: "Know the truth, and the truth will set you free." The truth that we find in meditation, of course, is that God is love—that there is a core spiritual presence in our lives that we can know directly by holding our focus to our hearts and opening to the inflow of love.

We let go of our fearful state by learning to be still, and in that stillness we come to know the truth, and in that state of alignment with the deeper reality of life, we discover the primal power of love as it animates us and connects us directly with the infinite Unnameable.

Pause and Experience

Pause again after reading this paragraph, let your eyes close . . . tune inward . . . feel the air flowing in and out of your nose . . . be aware of your hands . . . your feet . . . your face . . . allow your mind to become quiet . . . and in the middle of your breathing, focus on your own heart . . . and simply look inward . . . without judging . . . to know the truth . . . and open your heart . . . to love . . . as you say to yourself, "I love myself . . . I love the world . . ."

Love Your Neighbor as You Love Yourself

Jesus laid this seven-word exhortation on the world like a psychological bombshell. I remember when I first realized one implication of the statement: that in order to love my neighbor I must first of all love myself. It's important to note that when he told us how to love, Jesus realized fully that love is an inner quality that we nurture inside our own hearts, and that then flows out to those around us. If we try to love our neighbor but neglect to nurture our love for our own self, we're doomed. The first step in learning to love is making an inner connection between our hearts and the ultimate source of love.

The simple and ultimate resolution to the selfish-selfless polarity is found in contemplating Jesus' challenge to love our neighbors as much as we love ourselves. He didn't say, "Love your neighbor more than you love yourself," because he surely recognized that this is impossible. When there is no love in your heart, you have no love to give your neighbor. But as you increase the flow of love into your own heart, you increase the love you have available to flow out to your neighbor. In spite of various ongoing criticisms of meditation practice as inherently selfish, we can't escape the fact that, if we're to love those around us more, our first responsibility is to turn inward and become more loving in our relationship with our own selves.

In meditation as we're learning it, we take time each day to simply look inward, to watch our thoughts, to see how our negative thoughts generate negative emotions . . . and in the seeing, to choose not to think such thoughts that hurt us.

We are creatures who gravitate toward pleasure and avoid pain. When we see that certain judgmental thoughts cause us considerable and chronic pain, then we gravitate away from such thoughts. This is the healing power of meditation. When we see the truth clearly, we change. When we know the truth of our own self-damaging mental habits, we set ourselves free from those mental habits.

Choosing to Be Lovable

How can we use these three sayings from the Judeo-Christian tradition to help us choose love over fear? Let's begin by looking again at the sayings as they translate into meditation practice.

- *Fear not:* Learn to quiet chronic worries and judgments, hold your focus of attention in the present moment rather than the future, and don't be afraid to see your own self honestly and clearly. Choose to allow love rather than fear to fill your heart.

- *Be still:* Learn to quiet your mind at will. When you look inward and watch your own mental habits in action, don't judge them. Be still, as the observer or witness, and from the depths of that stillness . . .

- *Know the truth:* Learn to look directly and see who you are and what the truth of the matter is, and the truth will set you free.

That's the essence of emotional and cognitive healing when approached from a meditative understanding. To see the truth clearly and without judgment is to initiate growth, correction, and healing.

Pause in meditation, look inward, and observe how you're feeling about yourself. Say, "I love myself just as I am," and then see whether this is really true for you right now, or whether the statement unearths the presence of discord in your heart.

If you find that your mind is refusing to let you feel love in your heart for yourself, look honestly at the truth of the matter without being afraid of what you might find. Perhaps you find that you have a recurrent thought that you are not really lovable. You judge yourself as perhaps too ugly to be lovable, or not attractive sexually. You feel repulsion and judgment toward your own self. Or maybe you judge yourself to be stupid, or a clumsy oaf, or hopelessly lazy—or just basically a boring, depressing, bothersome person.

It's very important, if you come to this third expansion and find that your heart is somehow closed to loving yourself, that you just relax, stay aware of your breathing, and look clearly at what it is that your mind is thinking that makes you feel unlovable—catch your judgmental mind in action!

Once you've seen the negative mental attitudes that block your feeling of love for yourself, you are ready to look beyond your judgments of yourself to see the truth of the matter. Who are you really deep down? Is the judgment you hold in your mind true? Are you unable to let love flow into your heart? Or can you begin to focus on yourself as a creation of God and therefore perfectly okay just as you are?

As your mind becomes quiet in meditation and you begin to feel who you really are deep down, not as a personality or body but as a living spiritual being, you will gain direct knowledge of who you are. And in knowing the truth, you can choose to let love flow into your heart for yourself. That inflow of love will begin to heal your attitudes toward yourself so that a new sense of self-love can flourish within your heart.

Your relationship with yourself is your closest relationship. You are the one who chooses what kind of relationship that will be—a fearful, judging relationship or a loving relationship. Ask yourself in meditation what kind of friendship you want to nurture with your own self—do you want an inner friend who constantly judges you and denies you love, or do you want an inner friend who accepts you just as you are?

Within your core belief system developed in early childhood, you are holding on to an opinion of yourself as either lovable or unlovable. In the next days and weeks in meditation, when you come to the fourth meditation and say, "I love myself . . . ," I encourage you to:

1. Look carefully to see what old beliefs about yourself the meditation immediately activates—who is it inside you who evaluates and says, "Yes, you're lovable," or denies you the wonderful feeling of loving yourself?

2. Take time to consider what you yearn to feel in your heart when you say, "I love myself . . ."

3. Consider that at any given moment you are free to choose whether to continue fixating on what you don't like about yourself, or to go ahead and accept and love yourself just as you are.

From this moment forward, I challenge you to start a new habit of giving yourself permission to feel good in your heart toward your own self. It's up to you. Risk everything. Love yourself. Let the love that heals all flow in . . . and then you will be able to love others with this same love that flows into you.

Love Is Not an Idea

You'll find that you cannot make more love flow into your heart and out into the world by simply thinking about how much you want to do this. As long as your focus of attention is in your head, it is not in your heart. And conversely, you'll find that the more you choose to hold your mind's attention to your heart region and the less you focus higher up in your head, the more you'll be able to feel love.

Love is a feeling, not an idea—and feelings of love are felt primarily in the heart region, not in the head.

You might find that you encounter bad feelings when you turn toward your heart. We carry around old wounds of rejection and despair and hopelessness and anger in our hearts, and such wounds don't magically disappear. We cannot wipe out our past. We can only accept whatever has happened to us, and stop judging it as unacceptable or unforgivable or unbearable.

You'll find that the secret to opening your heart to love again is to learn to accept the total reality of your past. Don't resist or reject or deny feelings in your heart, whatever they are at the moment. Instead, accept them completely . . . and then choose to allow the healing light of love to shine upon them. This is the only way to transcend heartache . . . through loving yourself just as you are and letting God's love reach in and transform your inner experience. This is the love Jesus gave to his disciples and to everyone— unconditional love that forgives all.

Over and over in formal meditation, and also throughout your day, remember to say to yourself, "I love myself just as I am," and allow this potential for loving to awaken in your heart. Make the inner choice to accept yourself . . . and step by step you'll be able to look inward without judgment to see the deeper truth of who you are. In this meditative act, you'll soon discover that you are a perfect creation who does not need to be changed in order to be full of love—both for yourself and for those around you.

Pause and Reflect

After reading this paragraph, feel free to put the book aside and relax a bit . . . tune in to your breathing . . . your heart . . . and notice how you feel in your heart right now . . . toward yourself. Just look, and accept. Is it easy for you to choose to love yourself just as you are, without any hesitation or qualification . . . or do you carry negative judgments and attitudes and beliefs about yourself that shut off the flow of love into your heart? Take some time to reflect on how you respond or react when you say to yourself, "I love myself . . ."

As I Have Loved You

Jesus offered his disciples another gem of spiritual wisdom to help them understand how to walk the heart path. He offered them his own loving example as a model for loving each other. He said simply, "Love one another as I have loved you."

Jesus was surely a very loving human being, almost never getting angry, always turning the other cheek, being patient and kind and deeply compassionate and understanding of the thoughts and feelings of those around him. However, when we look closely at how Jesus loved those around him, we must accept that he did not manage his life so as to minimize the emotional pain of those around him. He didn't try to take care of other people's feelings. That wasn't what he considered love.

For him, love was first of all having his heart wide open all the time to his own spiritual core of being. In that constant meditative state of devotion, he seems to have lived not by plotting and manipulating with his logical mind, but by following his heart's wisdom and dictates as he felt moved moment to moment.

What was important to Jesus was to love God with all his heart, mind, and soul, and to do the work before him as he was spontaneously moved to do so. For instance, he told his disciples that when they were brought before the authorities, they weren't to think beforehand what they would say—they were to allow Spirit to speak through them while they held their hearts pure and tuned in to spiritual wisdom and guidance.

In other words, rather than living a life dictated by "shoulds" and "shouldn'ts," Jesus surrendered to reality and was always true to his own deeper calling, regardless of what other people thought of his actions, or how his actions affected other people's feelings. In all he did, from what we know, he lived the loving path of total surrender to the spiritual moment.

Jesus pointed out that he came neither to live by the laws of his culture nor to destroy them. He came to fulfill the law by teaching a few new laws that were of a qualitatively higher thrust—namely, to love our neighbors as we love ourselves and to love each other with the same fearless honesty and dedication to the truth as he did.

Forgiving All

To talk about love is to talk about forgiveness. Jesus as well as Mohammed taught that God is first and foremost a forgiving God and that this power of forgiveness is grounded in the power of love. One of Jesus' main messages during his two years of active teaching was to assure everyone who came to him with a sincere heart that God forgave them for everything they thought they had done wrong.

Theology in all religions is very much caught up in dualistic notions of right and wrong, of good and bad, of saints and sinners. But belief systems that judge us as good or bad are unnecessary and even irrelevant in meditation. The concept of sin and sinning doesn't enter into it because our aim in meditation is to let go of beliefs and judgment and simply tune in to our oneness with God. In the act of meditation we choose to stop judging ourselves entirely, and instead to accept ourselves just as we are.

However, we've all done things we feel bad about, and we sometimes continue to act in ways that hurt other people, especially when we're afraid and therefore defensive or antagonistic. We also tend to continue to judge ourselves for things we did a long time ago. Such judgments generated our beliefs about being bad people, hopeless sinners, and so forth. How do we deal with our feelings of being sinful and even evil when they arise in meditation? How do we forgive ourselves for "bad" things we have done, so that we can love ourselves unconditionally?

Forgiveness is built into the natural process of meditation, as we've already seen. The notion of good and evil, of being bad and sinning, is just that—a notion. Meditation takes us to a quality of consciousness where we let go of our thinking mind's judgments of our past behavior and enter into a state of grace where, rather than thinking about God's love and forgiveness, we experience directly in our hearts the inflow into our lives of God's acceptance and love.

Knowing from meditative experience that the infinite creative force of the universe and beyond is a loving force and therefore utterly forgiving, we approach the act of forgiveness in meditation from a pragmatic, psychological point of view. We look inward to see whether we are judging, denying, or condemning either our own selves or anyone around us as wrong, bad, evil, unworthy, unacceptable, or unlovable. If we find any such judgment or condemnation or refusal to accept reality just as it happened, we use the basic meditative approach to healing this judgment: we accept the reality of what happened as neither good nor bad but as just the reality of what happened—and in the act of letting go of judgment, we allow healing love to flow.

The same is true in how you relate in love or judgment with everyone around you. In the Gospel of Mark, Jesus offers several suggestions for both meditating and forgiving: "Whenever you stand praying, forgive, if you have anything against anyone, so that your Father who is in heaven will also forgive you your transgressions. For if you forgive others for their transgressions, your heavenly Father will also forgive you." A little later on he recommends that when you begin to pray you check on whether you're holding a grudge or other bad feeling in your heart for anyone—and if you are, to immediately go out and establish peace with this person before you continue with your prayers.

Thus, in our fourth meditation it's important to regularly pause when you say, "I love myself ... I love the world ..." and think about whether there's anyone you need to forgive. If so, in your heart and perhaps in person as well, depending on the situation, it's vital to your own peace of mind and spiritual experience to first accept the supposed injustice your mind thinks this person has done to you. Surrender to the reality of life. Accept and forgive. As you let go of your judgments against those around you, you will become loving toward them, in the same spirit that Jesus loved.

Learning to love ourselves is a lifelong exploration. Letting go of our fears and judgments is an ongoing effort that we continue with each new meditation session. This fourth expansion offers you the opportunity each new day to renew your choice to love yourself just as you are, and to heal any wounds or contractions that you find in your heart.

I want to emphasize that there's no real end point in this healing process. Meditation isn't goal-oriented. This moment, not the future, is always where our focus returns to, and each moment by definition is brand new . . . our entire sensory experience right now is being created by the unfolding physical manifestation of Spirit or the Tao or whatever name you give to the Unnameable. This eternal unending moment of the present is where our personal presence opens up and merges with the Greater Presence . . .

Jesus said, "The kingdom of heaven is at hand." Often translators insist that the more accurate translation is, "The kingdom of heaven is within." Both translations point to the here and now. This is where it's at. And meditation is our most direct way to regularly pause, open up, tune in, and enter that kingdom of heaven . . . where our hearts are continually inundated with love . . .

HEART AWAKENING: Guided Meditation 4

You'll notice that for the rest of the meditations in this book the beginning words remain the same. My intent is to provide you with the basic short sequence of words, the mantra, that you will move through each time you do the *Seven Masters* meditation so that you can truly learn it by heart. Then, each time you pause to meditate, you won't have to look up what to do. The structure and the verbal pointers will be a part of your natural world.

Make sure you're comfortable, sitting however you choose . . . make whatever movements you want to . . . and gently turn your attention to the air flowing in and out of your nose or mouth . . . expand your awareness to include the movements in your chest and belly as you breathe . . . say to yourself, "I'm breathing freely . . ."

Also at the same time, be aware of your heart, beating right in the middle of your breathing . . . be aware of your whole body, here in this present moment . . . your feet . . . your hands . . . your face . . . your whole being . . . be aware of the sounds around you . . . and now say to yourself, "My mind is quiet . . ."

Expand your awareness to include the world around you . . . your family . . . your friends . . . the people you work with . . . everyone . . . and everything they're doing right now . . . the world just as it is in this moment . . . God's perfect creation . . . and say to yourself, "I accept the world just as it is . . ."

And now turn your inner attention to your feelings of acceptance and love for yourself. Begin to notice how you feel in your heart, for your own self. To see how your respond to the words today, say a few times on the exhale, "I love myself just as I am . . . ," and see how you respond today to these words . . .

Don't judge yourself, regardless of what you feel in your heart right now toward yourself . . . just let the feelings be there . . . look at them . . . see the truth . . . are you relaxed into a feeling of love and inner acceptance? . . . or are you somehow fighting against yourself, unable to forgive and accept completely who you are in this moment? . . .

What would happen if you let go right now of all the fear and rejection in your heart for your own self? . . . Let all your thoughts quiet down ... be aware of your bodily sensations ... and at the same time, the sounds around you ... allow the feeling in your heart to begin to soften ... to relax ... begin to be open to the possibility of accepting and loving yourself just as you are ... observe ... are you afraid to open up and love yourself? ...

Stay with your breathing ... let the stillness deepen ... the thoughts fade away ... for at least a few moments, allow yourself to see yourself as perfectly okay just as you are ... you are God's creation ... love yourself as Jesus loved ... without judgment ... without fear ... without hesitation ... forgive yourself for everything ... and say again, "I love myself just as I am ..."

With thoughts quiet, just be with yourself, without judgment or fear ... look and see who you really are ... look to see the truth of who you are deep inside ... beyond words ... the direct experience ... within your heart ... and allow good feelings to begin to expand within your heart for yourself ... and outflowing to everyone you know ... let the love flow ...

It's your choice, to love yourself ... or not to. Look to your heart and see what you choose right now ... to judge and fear and reject yourself, or to open up, accept, and love yourself ... choose ...

As an act of self-love, you can choose to give yourself permission to feel good in your heart ... surrender to love ... let it fill you ...

"I love myself just as I am ..."

Let your meditation deepen ... let the love flow ...

FOR INSTANT STREAMED-AUDIO GUIDANCE, PLEASE GO TO
www.7masters.com

CHAPTER 5

Emotional Healing—Mohammed

A s we've seen, our meditation experience naturally begins with a full focus on what's happening in the present moment in our bodies . . . our breathing, our heartbeat, our whole-body presence . . . and our emotions, thoughts, intuitions, feelings, perceptions, and all the other ingredients of personal identity that, taken together, create our interior experience of being alive.

The first four expansions constitute one whole movement into full interior consciousness of who we are within our personal bubble of consciousness. When we expand our awareness to include everything that's happening in our sensory and cognitive realms, we find ourselves living within a bubble that reaches out as far as our various senses can tune in to the outside world.

For some people, especially those of a strong scientific bent, this personal level of consciousness expansion represents the entire meditative experience. If you find this to be true for yourself, then fine—you now have the four expansions as your long-term meditative practice.

However, my own experience in meditation has led me to understand that other expansions of consciousness become possible—when we choose to open our hearts to communion with an infinite transpersonal consciousness that exists beyond our personal bubble of meditative awareness.

This chapter and meditative expansion focus on the process by which we can choose to make our personal bubble of awareness permeable, and allow a greater spiritual presence and power to flow into our personal awareness. In traditional terminology, this inflow has been referred to as God's love, the touch of Allah's hand, or the union of our personal mind with the infinite Tao.

As we learn the meditative process for opening up to this expansion into transpersonal consciousness, we need to be careful not to conceptualize who this transpersonal God is, and what the relationship between our personal selves and the Greater Self might be. This is for you to find out for yourself, through direct experience. My job here is to give you the meditative tool that leads you right to the point of surrender and opening.

In my experience, there definitely does exist an infinite spiritual consciousness that permeates physical reality. And we are all capable in meditation of expanding our personal consciousness to merge with this transpersonal consciousness. The particular experience that comes to you when you make this expansion will be affected, of course, by your personal religious beliefs and expectations.

When you purposefully expand your meditation experience beyond your biological energetic awareness to include the infinite, you engage in a spiritual leap of faith in which you make yourself utterly vulnerable and receptive to a power, wisdom, love, and consciousness that transcends your individual experience, and connects you directly with enlightened dimensions of being. This choice to merge with a consciousness that transcends your personal consciousness is so vital that we'll be exploring the process throughout the final three expansions of this meditation program.

Pause and Reflect

Perhaps you'd like to pause for a few moments now . . . and let the verbal dust settle a bit . . . tune in to your breathing . . . your heart . . . your whole body here in this present moment . . . and begin to explore how you feel about opening your heart to the inflow of love and guidance from beyond your personal sensory bubble of awareness . . . just observe, don't judge . . ., as we begin this exploration of your capacity to merge your personal awareness with the Universal Consciousness . . .

Open to Receive

The focus phrase for this fifth expansion is one that I'm always thankful to arrive at, because almost always I experience a most remarkable shift in consciousness just by saying the words: "My heart is open . . . to receive . . . God's healing help."

This is usually said as a three-breath statement to allow you to go deeply into each phrase before moving into the next. The first two phrases are primal and short, delivering the subject ("my heart") and the verb ("is open") and the intent ("to receive"). The third part of the statement, as we'll see later in this chapter, is more complex and can be modified to suit your preference regarding what to call the creative loving force of the universe—and also the quality of inflow that you feel you most need at the moment.

For some of you, the term "God" works very well. For others, especially those in the Taoist and Buddhist modes, or those who take the secular scientific perspective, another term of your own choosing may be preferable. You'll want to experiment and see what specific word or words feel best for you as you turn your mind's attention beyond the confines of your own mind, and toward communion with whatever the reality of spiritual presence in the universe is for you.

By saying this three-part statement of intent, you are actively encouraging your heart to open up and become permeable so that your personal soul will be touched by the universal spiritual presence. This chapter will shed beautiful light on our potential for a seamless relationship with the spiritual dimensions that lie beyond our personal senses and awareness.

This fifth expansion on the *Seven Masters* odyssey will surprise you each time you move through it. For the rest of your life you'll find yourself exploring the power of this expansion to merge your personal life with the Infinite Consciousness, of which you are a tiny but highly significant part.

The act of surrendering to a greater spiritual presence and will has always been the foundation of the Muslim faith and experience, and in this chapter we will learn a great deal from the Muslim approach to meditation. Let's begin by taking a look at the life of Mohammed, the founder of Islam.

Approaching Mohammed

Just as we have major difficulties getting the historic facts straight on Patanjali, Lao Tzu, Buddha, and Jesus, historians have found Mohammed an equally elusive figure, especially when trying to develop a clear sense of who he was as a spiritual teacher.

Mohammed was born around 560 A.D. in Mecca, which at that time was a small Arab trading city located at a large oasis a two-day camel-trip south of Jerusalem and Damascus. Long before Mohammed appeared, the Old Testament prophet Abraham and his son Ishmael were said to have created a holy site, called Ka'aba and dedicated to Yahweh, at the oasis of Zamzam, which lies at the heart of Mecca.

Ishmael's descendants would become various Arab tribes, most of whom gradually lost their identity with the Hebrew tradition. But the Jewish presence and influence in Mecca dates back far into antiquity, and there were still many Jews living and practicing their faith in Mecca and nearby Medina when Mohammed was born. Certainly the general notion that there was one Almighty God above and beyond all the various local deities worshiped by different tribes of the area, was common during Mohammed's childhood. However, what the Jews considered pagan worship of a great many *jinn* spirits and idols was running rampant in the city.

Six hundred years after the birth of the Christian religious movement, several Christian sects were residing in the Arab region, most notably the Nestorian sect. Although illiterate himself, Mohammed clearly had contact with both Jewish and Christian beliefs during his childhood and early adulthood, and as an Arab perceived himself as a descendant of the original Adam-Abraham-Ishmael religious tradition.

Mohammed would integrate a great deal of both Jewish and Christian teachings and beliefs into his new, uniquely Arab-language religion. However, he also established Islam as clearly distinct in certain major theological ways, as we'll explore in a moment.

Mohammed's father was from the locally dominant Quraish tribe, which was subdivided into a dozen autonomous clans. His father was a poor but solid trader who died on a caravan journey when Mohammed was still in his mother's womb. Mohammed's mother, Amina, also died, when her child was just six years old. In his later adult life, Mohammed would place special emphasis on providing adequate care for orphans, widows, and poor people in general.

In his teen years, Mohammed was raised mostly by his uncle Abd Manaf and his extended trading family based in Mecca. Tales and myths abound about Mohammed's childhood, but almost nothing has been historically documented. He seems to have grown up as an especially honest and trustworthy young man, working in the caravan-trade business. We're told that he had an unusual power of inspiring confidence and assuming responsibility. Around the age of twenty-five he took over the fortunes of a beautiful and wealthy widow named Kadijah, who was fifteen years his senior. They grew close in all ways, and soon they were married and raising a family.

Mohammed went each year into retreat in the desert near Mount Hira for the holy month of Ramadan, to focus on solitary spiritual meditation. One fateful year, according to Islamic scripture, he was suddenly struck while meditating with a series of visions that would forever change not only his own life, but ultimately the lives of over one billion human beings.

In the Koran it is recorded that Mohammed saw a vision of the Jewish angel Gabriel and other angels as well: "I awoke from my sleep, and it was as if they had written a message in my heart. I went out of the cave and while I was on the mountain, I heard a voice saying, 'O Mohammed, you are Allah's Apostle, and I am Gabriel.'"

From this initial revelation and others to follow, Mohammed received a steadily growing body of statements from "beyond" that he memorized and began teaching to a growing band of followers in Mecca. His wife was his first convert to the new spiritual vision coming through him, and during the next ten years he continued to receive inspired statements that would ultimately become the Koran, or Qur'an, the sacred scripture of Islam.

As the years went by, Mohammed became more and more certain of his identity as a prophet in the direct lineage of the ancient Hebrew prophets. He considered Jesus the most recent prophet from Allah and was utterly respectful of Jesus' teachings, but he refused to consider Jesus more than a prophet. Mohammed was very clear that worshiping Jesus as Allah's only begotten son was idolatry. In the Koran he says that "the Messiah, Jesus son of Mary, was only an envoy of God. So believe in God and the envoys of God, and do not speak of a trinity. God alone is the One worthy of worship." This insistence naturally distanced Mohammed from the Christian communities in the area.

Although he was dead set against any form of idolatry that took one's focus from Allah, Mohammed made a definite point a number of times in the Koran of saying: "Be they Muslims, Christians, Jews, or Sabians, those who believe in God and the Last Day and who do good have their reward with their Lord." Islam in this regard is inclusive, and indeed at first it wasn't seen as a separate religion at all, but as a fulfillment of the teachings of the earlier prophets. The Koran specifically says: "We believe in God and what was revealed to us and what was revealed to Abraham and Ishmael, Isaac and Joseph and the Tribes, and what was given to Moses and Jesus, and what was given to the prophets from their Lord, and we do not make any distinction between individuals among them, for we submit to God."

However, the Jewish community in Mecca didn't accept the young man claiming to be the new prophet of God. Instead, they tended to make fun of him, and along with the ruling Arab population in Mecca, they eventually forced him to flee the city— finally in fear of his life. Losing most of his accumulated wealth, he fled with his family to nearby Medina, where two Jewish communities and three Arab tribes rather uncomfortably shared a fortified city.

During his first few years in Medina, Mohammed continued with his teaching and found himself being rapidly accepted as a spiritual leader In a decade his growing popularity and power had made him the dominant leader of the city. After a number of small skirmishes with neighboring Mecca, whose leaders refused to let him and his followers make pilgrimages to the shrine of Abraham, he entered the city with an army and forcefully claimed his new religious movement's right to visit the holy shrine.

Mohammed and Meditation

Even after he regained his wealth, Mohammed lived a simple life. He seemed humble, friendly, and consistently kind (except when leading an army into battle). He was devoted to his several wives, to ensuring a safe, poverty-free community, and to preaching a faith quite similar to the Christian faith—namely, that Allah is the one true God, that Allah is all-merciful and all-wise, and that total surrender to this ultimate God and tuning in to and doing God's will is the true spiritual path.

Of key importance to our ability to trust and open up to a higher spiritual force in our lives, Mohammed taught, Allah is first and foremost an all-loving God, whose blessing and guidance are always available to those who open to his presence. Allah is also ready to readily forgive all sins of those who are penitent and ask for forgiveness. Mohammed taught that we should have no fear about opening our hearts and allowing God's influence and love to come flowing into our lives.

In reaction to the general carousing and blood-for-blood ethics of the local Arab community at the time, the morality of the rapidly expanding Islamic Empire in Mecca and Medina was fairly strict. Islam emphasized living a good, fair life as outlined in Moses' Ten Commandments and walking a middle path without going to extremes, while constantly holding God's name and guiding presence in one's mind.

The primary religious practice that Mohammed taught was the performance of regular ritual prayer, called *salat.* Originally the daily meditative practice was to pause three times a day and recite verses of the Koran while performing certain humbling movements and prayerful bowings to Allah. Mohammed in the Koran emphasized that this type of ritual prayer had been practiced by Abraham, Ishmael, Moses, and Jesus and was to stand as the operational heart of the specifically Arab religion he was bringing into being.

A primary teaching throughout the Koran, repeated over and over by the faithful in ritual prayer, is the fact that "God wants to give you clarity and guide you, and to be present for you . . . for God is most knowing, most wise . . . God wants to lighten your burden, knowing that humanity was created weak." In other words, God is always present to enter our hearts and guide us with his infinite wisdom and knowledge, because otherwise in our human routines and mental habits we tend to lose touch with our deeper spiritual awareness and fall into upsetting thoughts and behavior.

This primary focus of the Islamic faith—continual faith and trust in "opening to God"—leads us directly into the theme of this chapter and meditative expansion, namely, the focus statement: "My heart is open . . . to receive . . . God's healing help." In the Islamic tradition, God already knows what is in our hearts, and we don't have to tell Allah what help we need. All we need to do is call on God, by whatever name, surrender our ego center to our spiritual center, and shift from broadcast to receive mode. As I understand it, this is what Muslims are doing at a spiritual level five times a day when they pause for ritual prayer.

Mohammed said in the Koran, or rather he quotes an angel as saying: "God is the first and the last, the manifest and the hidden . . . God is with you all wherever you may be, and God sees what you do . . . God knows what is in all hearts." Therefore, not only in the ritual prayers each day but in every moment of one's life, the true spiritual response to God's presence is to hold one's heart open to receive God's guidance. This is the one and only meditation in the Islamic tradition as I see it—to continually surrender our ego intent to God's higher spiritual intent and thus to allow God's healing love and wisdom to flow into our lives, continually in every waking moment.

Quieting the Chatterbox

Beyond the ultimate meditative aim of continually bringing God's presence into our lives, very little is said specifically about meditation in the Koran. The Arabic term *Islam* translates most clearly as "surrender to the will of God." Holding God in one's mind, and being open in full surrender to respond to God's will and guidance, *is* meditation in the Islamic tradition.

An expert in Islamic studies recently reminded me that the Arabic meaning of the word "thought" is usually translated as "worry." As we've seen in earlier chapters, a primary aim of meditation is to move our focus of attention beyond worrying thoughts and into direct communion with the love of God that flows into us when we quiet our worrying mind. By surrendering the destiny of our lives to God, we tap into a higher guidance that enables us to relax, and trust our deeper guidance to move us through life without having to worry chronically about the future.

This act of quieting the chatterbox of the everyday mind is accomplished in the Islamic tradition by filling the mind with spiritual sayings—repeating these sayings silently to oneself or sometimes saying them out loud. And what is the intent of these sayings? There is only one intent—to point the mind toward direct encounter and communion with God.

The seven one-line focus phases that constitute the heart of our *Seven Masters* meditation program serve the same higher purpose. Indeed, our meditation program at this level directly reflects the Islamic approach to meditation. In each meditation session I encourage you to say, in order, the seven statements of intent that point your mind's attention toward your greater spiritual presence.

We'll explore in later chapters how you can also repeat just one of our seven sayings, over and over with each new breath, in much the same way the Islamic community repeats certain sayings from the Koran, Buddhists repeat certain sayings of Buddha, or Christians repeat certain sayings of Jesus. This process of filling your mind with particular words and ideas that point you toward God, by whatever name, will consistently fulfill your meditative intent.

Pause and Experience

Take a few moments away from reading to experiment with the process of repeating a spiritual statement over and over . . .

saying it to yourself on the exhale . . . out loud or more subliminally, as you prefer . . . and then being silent on the inhale
. . . you might want to see what comes to you as you say, "My
heart is open . . . to receive . . . ," for twelve to twenty breaths.

Trance or Meditation

There are at least two distinctions to be made between traditional forms of ritual prayer and the meditation program we're
learning here. The seven sayings I'm encouraging you to repeat are
clearly not part of any particular religious theology or dogma, but
are more universal. The other distinction has to do with how the
sayings are repeated. In my study of hypnosis and trance states, I've
learned that by repeating one saying over and over again on each
new breath, people can move into a trance state where personal ego
identity is lost entirely and an often beautiful state of blissful transcendence is attained. This often happens in traditional ritual
prayer ceremonies dominated by verbal repetition.

There's a certain spiritual value to such a trance state, in that it
allows you to experience being conscious without your personal
ego being dominant. We all tend to move into this state and love it
when we get out on the dance floor, when we sing songs we know
by heart, when we go jogging, and so forth. The temporary eupho-
ria of entering into a trance state is definitely alluring and often a
great and much-needed relief from normal consciousness.

But I've found that moving into a trance state by whatever
means just isn't at all the same as moving into a meditative state
where we remain fully conscious in the unfolding present moment.
Many dimensions of consciousness are lost when we're in trance,
even in deep religious trances. In contrast, in a meditative state
we remain quietly aware of everything happening around us and

everything that comes spontaneously into our consciousness from deeper spiritual dimensions.

When I encourage you to move through the seven sayings or to repeat just one of them a number of times, the aim is to allow the words to aim your attention toward what they suggest. Once your attention is aimed in the desired direction, it's time to quiet your mind and simply *be in the experience* that comes to you as you move beyond all words into pure consciousness of the eternal present moment.

Surrendering

In our culture surrendering is usually considered an act of weakness; to surrender is to quit, to lose, to have your integrity along with your territory overrun. We're taught to do just the opposite of surrender—to fight the good fight, to never give up our personal ego-center to another power. Otherwise, we'll lose our integrity, we'll be trampled on by the victor, we'll experience failure and humiliation. The ego sees its job as protecting us from outside influences that would take us over, lead us astray, damage us, or otherwise disturb our inner equilibrium and belief regarding how things should be. The ego's job is to maintain the status quo, strengthen our sense of who we are, and fortify the beliefs and attitudes that we consider the foundation of our existence.

Spiritual awakening requires a surrender of the ego to a higher consciousness, a higher power, a greater reality than that contained in our ingrained beliefs about what life is all about. When we enter into meditation, we're expressing the desire to move beyond the programmed ideas and attitudes so as to encounter reality more directly as an experience in the present moment. We're seeking the truth beyond our prejudices. We're asking for the transformation of our sense of self through the experience of direct encounter with reality.

Where does this new expanded experience come from? Not

from our own concepts of reality, but rather from a source beyond our ego's definition and control. This is why the fifth expansion is so crucial to a complete meditative experience—because we're now at the point psychologically where we're ready to say the explosive words: "My heart is open . . . to receive. . . ."

The act of opening our hearts to receive love and wisdom is the true act of spiritual adventure. When we open our hearts to receive, we're making ourselves vulnerable by placing ourselves in a posture of submission, of trust. We're yielding our ego defenses and welcoming the experience of the flow of some greater power, some source of love and creation into our personal lives.

Surrendering our ego defenses and opening up to receive the inflow of a higher consciousness lies at the center of spiritual life. Psychologically, we've all been conditioned very strongly to be closed to outside influences that might threaten our ego's established sense of what life's all about.

However, as we're beginning to learn, our ego isn't a totally defensive and selfish quality of consciousness. The ego has experienced time and again momentary lapses of ego dominance when an unchecked inflow of intuitive, mystic, spiritual awareness occurred and the experience proved positive, not negative.

We have all been influenced by these occasional momentary lapses in ego control, when Spirit has rushed into our personal consciousness. Our hearts were touched to the quick by the experience. It is during such momentary lapses in ego control that we realize that we want to take this risk, we want to open our hearts and receive.

Where Faith Comes In

When we begin to risk opening our hearts to receive God's healing touch, using whatever words we choose, we're performing a leap of faith. The act of surrender requires that we feel enough trust in our hearts toward the source of the inflow, that we are willing to make our hearts vulnerable. We must have faith that the power we're welcoming into our core of being is good, loving, wise, and utterly trustworthy.

By definition, the spiritual inflow we're opening to is mysterious and beyond our conceptual understanding. We're asking to be overwhelmed by a reality that lies beyond our mind's intellectual concepts. That's what "spiritual" means after all—the greater reality that lies beyond our mind's conceptual model of reality.

On the one hand, we want to experience life more fully and tune in to "the truth that passes all understanding," as the Bible puts it. We all seem to have a built-in hunger to open up and merge with the infinite consciousness from whence our individual consciousness originated, as the scientists in *Why God Won't Go Away* have demonstrated with their brain research. But if this is so, why aren't we all already fulfilling this desire and living our lives wide open to spiritual guidance and empowerment?

Most of us have a certain faith based on past positive encounters with the divine. That faith encourages us to make the leap and open up, to surrender and become vulnerable. But an equal and opposite force within us obviously stands directly in the way of this openness to spiritual surrender and transcendence. What is this equal and opposite force that so often keeps us from risking the ultimate spiritual act?

Pause and Reflect

You might want to take a few moments right now to pause and reflect on your own level of faith in surrendering to the inflow of spiritual energy and love . . .

- Do you trust the spiritual universe enough to make yourself vulnerable to its inflow?

- Are you open to receive, or are you closed down?

- What is it you fear that tends to keep your heart closed to spiritual inflow?
- Are you ready and willing to open your heart to the spiritual unknown?

Emotional Healing

Mohammed said over and over in the Koran that when you point your attention toward God, God comes to you—a God who is all-loving as well as all-powerful and all-wise. When you say to yourself, "My heart is open to receive God's healing help," you are quite specifically pointing your heart's attention directly toward the ultimate source of positive spiritual guidance and healing love.

We've seen that the primary reason we stay closed off to spiritual experience is that we carry in our thoughts and emotions a whole assortment of contractions and wounds from earlier days— wounds that keep us fearful, suspicious, untrusting, and defensive. If we don't heal these wounds, we tend to remain closed off to our higher spiritual potential.

We were all damaged one way or the other while growing up. It seems impossible to get through childhood without having our feelings seriously hurt quite often, and without developing inhibitions and contractions. To be born a human on this earth carries the guarantee that you'll be banged around and wounded emotionally. As adults, we either manage to heal those emotional wounds— or go through life constricted, limited, uptight, and suffering.

Each time you enter into the *Seven Masters* meditation process and come to this fifth expansion, you're entering into a state of mind where you can actively open your heart with all its wounds and contractions, and receive the healing touch of universal love. Having at least temporarily surrendered your ego's almighty control over your destiny, you're ready to open up to a higher order of clarity, healing, and realization. Your ego is making the selfless act of getting out of the way so that deep emotional and spiritual healing can take place.

Let's review this process again, because it's so basic, so simple, and yet often so easily forgotten:

1. You choose to enter into meditation, and you move through the first four steps of the expansion process.

2. You turn your focus of attention to your heart and experience honestly whatever emotions or attitudes are dominating your heart and perhaps need to be healed.

3. You accept what you find in your heart rather than deny it (even if it hurts).

4. You choose to open your heart to the inflow of God's healing love to directly touch and heal the emotional wound or fearful mental attitude or belief.

Whenever you turn your attention to your heart and find that it aches, that it feels contracted or numb or not even there, be assured that you can move through the fifth expansion and immediately open your heart to receive direct healing love from the ultimate healing source. If you hurt inside emotionally, be it with heartbreak or disappointment, anger or fear, grief or despair, just say the magic words and you've activated the most powerful natural spiritual healing system: "My heart is open to receive . . . God's healing help."

Please feel free to understand this healing process within whatever theological or philosophical framework you prefer. The ultimate source of the healing will be the same, regardless of whether you label it God or Allah or your Higher Self or Great Spirit or the healing power of love in the universe. The healing is empowered not by what you call it but by your choice to open your heart to receive.

Of course, sometimes you'll enter into the fifth expansion not feeling any pain or anguish at all in your heart. Indeed, by the time you reach the fifth expansion, especially after you've been doing this meditation daily for a while, you'll often be feeling very good indeed. When this is the case, you might want to replace the phrase "God's healing help" with one of these variations: "My heart is open . . . to receive spiritual insight . . . to receive strength and guidance . . . to receive love . . . to receive whatever is coming right now to me . . . (or simply) to receive . . ."

Mohammed told his followers that they had only to turn their minds and hearts to Allah, and Allah would heal and guide and bless them. Jesus likewise said those beautiful words: "Ask and it shall be given to you, seek and you will find, knock and it will open. . . ."

With this fifth expansion, this is what you are doing. You're directly asking God for help. You're knocking on heaven's door . . . and welcoming whatever flow comes into your heart from this ultimate spiritual source. As the old folk say, "It don't get no better than that." We're all blessed to have such instant access to the ultimate divine. Our main challenge is simply to remember to ask.

EMOTIONAL HEALING: Guided Meditation 5

Make sure you're comfortable, sitting however you choose . . . make whatever movements you want to . . . and gently turn your attention to the air flowing in and out of your nose or mouth . . . expand your awareness to include the movements in your chest and belly as you breathe . . . say to yourself, "I'm breathing freely . . ."

Also be aware of your heart, right in the middle of your breathing . . . be aware of your whole body, here in this present moment . . . your feet . . . your hands . . . your face . . . your whole being . . . be aware of the sounds around you . . . and say to yourself, "My mind is quiet . . ."

Expand your awareness to include the world around you
. . . the people in your family . . . your community . . . the
people you work with . . . everyone and everything they're
doing right now . . . the world just as it is in this moment . . .
God's perfect creation . . . and say to yourself, "I accept the
world, just as it is . . ."

And as you now hold your attention to your heart, notice
how you feel toward your own self . . . observe whether you
feel light or heavy in your heart . . . contracted or expansive
. . . if you're judging yourself, let the judgments go . . . forgive
yourself for everything that needs forgiving . . . just let the love
flow . . . say to yourself, "I love myself just as I am . . ."

Be aware of your breathing . . . your heart . . . your whole-
body presence . . . and the perceptual bubble of awareness that
you're living within all your life . . . and now begin to be aware
of where your personal awareness meets the infinite awareness
of the universe . . . the loving presence of God . . . see how it
feels today to say a few times, "My heart is open . . ."

Begin to allow your heart to open up and expand beyond
your personal bubble of love and life *so that you touch intimately* the infinite reality beyond you . . . gently, knowing
that you're opening to spiritual inflow, begin to allow your
personal membrane of awareness to become permeable . . .
and say to yourself a few times, "My heart is open . . . to receive . . ."

However you conceive or call the infinite spiritual presence
of the universe, God or Allah or the Tao or whatever . . .
begin to open your heart to this all-loving presence . . . and
say to yourself, "My heart is open to receive . . . God's healing
help . . ."

Our emotions are always in the process of letting go, of
healing, of recovering from past abuses and wounds . . . now is
the time to admit that you do sometimes hurt emotionally . . .
and that you would love to receive the touch of God in your

heart to help you to let go of the past, to forgive and recover
. . . to heal . . .

Let your fears go . . . let your beliefs go . . . let everything go
. . . surrender to the healing help that is now flowing into your
heart . . . into your whole being . . . knowing what you need
. . .

"My heart is open to receive . . . God's healing help . . ."
And now, allow your meditation go where it will . . .

FOR INSTANT STREAMED-AUDIO GUIDANCE, PLEASE GO TO
www.7masters.com

CHAPTER 6

Self-Remembering—Gurdjieff

Ifind myself laughing as we move into this sixth expansion of our meditation program, because with the end of each chapter so far it has felt as if we now had a complete meditation program—and yet with each new chapter we discover yet another crucial expansion of consciousness that is both possible and in many ways absolutely essential for a unified path of spiritual awakening.

I'm sure many of you feel that by learning the fifth expansion you now have all the necessary instruction for a lifetime of deep meditation. At many levels this is true. Once you've reached the inner expansion of consciousness where your heart is openly receiving direct inflow from the divine, perhaps there's no further expansion of consciousness necessary or even possible . . . or is there?

While studying at the San Francisco Theological Seminary and looking to the heart of my family's Christian heritage, I found myself going deeper and deeper into experiences of the fourth and fifth expansions as I opened my heart more fully both to loving myself and to receiving the inflow of spiritual love from the Source. As I delved further into the heart-centered contemplative tradition of the early Church, I felt certain I'd discovered the end-all of meditative programs. Letting the power of love flow in and the gift of love flow out seemed all-inclusive and utterly fulfilling.

At that time, in the early 1970s, the seminary was attempting to move with the times and expand its Christian orientation to embrace all true spiritual teachers. In this spirit the school offered to let me and a friend arrange evening courses on campus where non-Christian spiritual teachers could present their approaches to loving more deeply through contemplation and meditation. And so it came to pass that each Monday for a year we enjoyed a yoga class with Yogananda's primary disciple, Kriyananda. On Wednesdays we were blessed to have the powerful Sufi teacher Sam Lewis lead a large group in dancing, chanting, and meditation. And on Friday nights Alan Watts guided and instructed us in his mostly Zen Buddhist approach to meditation. To round off the week, one of the more avant-garde seminary professors led us in contemplative meditation in the Christian tradition on Sunday evenings.

In retrospect, I owe a great deal of the initial insights of this book to that special time. Such regular deep immersion in four distinct meditation traditions—Hindu, Sufi, Buddhist, and Christian—was an excellent way to explore the reality of meditation beyond any particular religious boundaries.

First Encounter

It was during one of our very popular Wednesday evening celebrations with Sam Lewis that I first heard the name Gurdjieff and learned about a meditation called "self-remembering." Sam himself was from traditional Jewish roots and had thus moved quite naturally into a strong Sufi orientation, since the Sufi tradition emerged out of the ancient teachings of both Jewish and Muslim masters. A truly enlightened American then in his seventies, Sam had been guided to his personal awakening many years before by Hazrat Inayat Khan, the renowned Sufi teacher and musical

SELF-REMEMBERING — GURDJIEFF • 141

master from India, and also by Nyogen Senzaki, founder of the first Zen monastery in America, and Swami Papa Ramdas of the Hindu tradition.

It was clear to everyone who met him that "Sufi Sam" embodied the new spiritual awakening that was dawning in the sixties. For many years he had been quietly teaching and studying; then, during his final years of life, he came rapidly into public prominence as he created the Sufi Islamia Ruhaniat Society and began receiving a series of visions, from which emerged the Dances of Universal Peace. These dances have since become the worldwide cornerstone of a wonderful and joyous spiritual community.

One evening during the winter of 1969, while leading the weekly Sufi dance for about two hundred people at the seminary, Sam began talking about a radical spiritual teacher named Gurdjieff and the essential meditative practice that he taught his disciples, called "self-remembering."

I recall Sufi Sam saying toward the end of his evening talk, "It's not enough to go around being loving and having an open heart. What's required on the spiritual path is to be aware of yourself going around with your heart open." At first I didn't understand what he was talking about. He explained that we must strive to be aware "both of our inner self, and what we're viewing, at the same time." He called this dual awareness "divided attention"—the practice of holding one part of one's attention outward in one's experience of the present moment, and holding the other part inward, toward the perceiving presence of the viewer.

"I'm talking Gurdjieff here, one of the true masters of the process," Sam told us. "He's the one who understood divided attention and self-remembering the very best. In fact, they're his terms."

He then dropped us down to a quiet meditation in which he guided us into a taste of divided attention. Then we moved into the pure pleasure of ritual dancing, which went on for another hour or so. Afterward, still mystified by the "self-remembering" process, I talked to Sam some more, and he gave me the phone number of an elderly woman who had studied in Paris with Gurdjieff himself in the thirties. She would be willing, he told me, to pass on what she'd learned from the master.

What she gently but firmly taught me in the months to come was that there is indeed a major step beyond our fifth expansion— the seemingly simple yet ultimately sublime step of learning to become conscious in two directions at once, aware of both outer and inner. She taught that dual focusing is the key to "being in the flow while also being conscious of who is experiencing the flow."

As she taught, all too often in meditation we tend to lose ourselves in spiritual experience. For Gurdjieff, this loss of consciousness was an indulgence rather than an expansion. Gurdjieff taught the seriously mature spiritual step of not losing oneself in one's spiritual experience, but rather using spiritual experience to clarify one's own inner presence.

In the fifth expansion we focused on experiencing the inflow of spiritual love and wisdom. Gurdjieff would have us expand this experience another notch through the inner act of turning part of our attention away from the observed experience and toward the observer. In other words, he would have us remember to focus on the perceiver—our own source of awareness.

Gurdjieff Himself

There are more than fourteen thousand websites related to this mysterious man, his life, and his teachings. Some of them are downright, and perhaps overly, worshipful; many are mostly unbiased and shed considerable light on who Gurdjieff was and how he continues to influence interested seekers; and some sites are openly hostile to him. Although Gurdjieff was deeply loved by a great many people, he seems to have purposefully created for the media a whirlwind of confusion and mystery around his life and his teachings.

Gurdjieff openly disdained all the spiritual groupies, celebrities, and media hounds who pursued him during his extremely active and colorful lifetime, and he often chased people away from his circle by appearing bizarre and even threatening. He regularly "violated all our preconceptions of a spiritual leader and sometimes repelled the more frivolous religious seekers," as one member of his group commented. He smoked and drank and cursed and partied and at times displayed the full range of human emotions. He loved to cook great feasts and was known for his celebrations and musical evenings that often went until three or four in the morning.

Gurdjieff was heard to say that "we never reach the limits of our strength," and indeed, he seldom seemed to. Numerous reports indicate that he'd usually slept only two hours a night. Typically he'd go to sleep around four in the morning, then come down around six from his hotel room in Paris, London, New York, or elsewhere and welcome conversations in his "office" at a nearby café. He was also a great dancer and musician, scored a number of operas, and created many ritual dances.

In spite of his growing media reputation as someone who went out of his way to outrage interviewers and hangers-on, Gurdjieff had a free and easy laugh and a great sense of humor. He was also both tender (he regularly found time to play and instruct the children in his large group of followers) and fearless, even in moments of extreme danger.

From the many accounts of people who were close to him, Gurdjieff emerges as a mysterious yet marvelous person. We know that he was born to Christian Armenian parents in the obscure town of Kars on the Russo-Turkish border near Alexandropol, probably in 1866 or thereabouts. According to his adventurous youthful autobiography, *Meeting with Remarkable Men,* he seems to have come from a scholarly family with a strong mystic bent. From an early age he aggressively sought out spiritual teachers of all kinds to whet his insatiable appetite for new information and insights. His interests and intellect were veracious: he could talk

144 • SEVEN MASTERS, ONE PATH

deeply about the theory of relativity and in the same conversation discuss yak raising in Nepal. He also seems to have been equally comfortable with movie stars and illiterate peasants.

Although Gurdjieff refused to write down, beyond his one early book, any concrete facts about his early life, it's fairly certain that he spent considerable time in India and Tibet and thereabouts, seeking training and insights into the ancient wisdom. In 1904 he was spotted in Tibet by Achmed Abdullah, a spy for the British the year they invaded that country. Gurdjieff was serving at the time as a crafty chief political officer to the Dalai Lama under the name Dordjieff. Some years later that same spy, by then a well-known author, saw Gurdjieff in New York and exclaimed, "That's him, that's Dordjieff!"

From 1910 through 1917, Gurdjieff was in Moscow and Petrograd, where he first appeared as a public figure, working diligently as both a controversial teacher with numerous students, and a musical composer. Then, just before the violence of the Russian Revolution broke out, he left Russia and crossed the Caucasus Mountains to Tiflis, moving from town to town westward, working at various jobs, and always teaching and exploring.

In 1922 he moved from Berlin to France, where he set up his Institute for the Harmonious Development of Man at the Chateau du Prieure. Achieving more and more recognition for his pioneering spiritual work, in 1924 he first visited America, giving public demonstrations with his students of his sacred dances, holding court at hotels in New York and Chicago, and continuing his nonstop teaching and all-night celebrations.

When he returned to France, he plunged back into his teaching of up to one hundred students at his institute, but then suffered injuries from a terrible auto accident that at least temporarily put an end to his teaching routine. Instead, he wrote several books, such as *Meetings with Remarkable Men; Beelzebub's Tales to His Grandson; Views from the Real World; The Herald of Coming Good;* and *Life Is Real Only Then.* His writings are challenging, and luckily his teachings are illuminated in other books written by his followers, most notably P. D. Ouspensky (sometimes spelled Uspenskii), G. I Bennett, Maurice Nicolle, and Robert Earl Burton.

Gurdjieff weathered the Second World War in Paris, where he managed to continue undisturbed with his teachings and general celebratory lifestyle without getting involved in the war scene whatsoever. In one account, he decided that he wanted to go to a German monastery to read through an ancient manuscript. With several dozen followers, he simply walked through the German lines one night. Firsthand reports say that the soldiers temporarily laid down their arms and watched, and none of Gurdjieff's group was in any way accosted or harmed during their crossing or during their return some days later.

Many other reports (fabled or otherwise) tell of a life spent without inhibition, fear, or deference to societal rules. Gurdjieff spent loads of money yet almost always seemed to have plenty of money flowing through his hands. He often paid the hotel and restaurant bills for dozens of his followers, cooked for them, and tipped on a fabulous scale. Yet he himself didn't bother to live a luxurious life. He was just that kind of guy.

Self-Remembering

I've painted Gurdjieff as a colorful, fun-loving, adventuresome extrovert, and indeed he was. However, he was also a ruthless instructor in "the Work," as he called it, and guided his disciples with a strong hand toward their own awakening. If you want to delve into Gurdjieff's teachings, you'll want to set aside considerable (and well-spent) time to study such books as Ouspensky's monumental *In Search of the Miraculous: Fragments of an Unknown Teaching* and Robert Earl Burton's meditative text *Self-Remembering*. Our purpose here is to learn the meditation that lies at the heart of Gurdjieff's teachings.

You're sitting here right now reading this book. You've learned to stay aware (more or less) of your breathing while you read. You've learned how to expand your awareness to include your whole body in the present moment. You're getting better and better at being conscious of all the perceptual inputs happening inside and around you that ground you in the immediacy of the present moment. You've started mastering the skill of choosing where to focus your power of attention. You're discovering ways to focus on your heart, to love yourself and those around you without judgment, and to open up to the flow of spiritual love and insight into your heart and mind.

As you're focusing your mind's attention to experience rewarding perceptions, this sixth expansion gently challenges you to also focus at least part of your attention in exactly the opposite direction—to look inward directly to your own source. By looking to the inner, transcendent source of your personal awareness, you'll quite naturally and effortlessly find yourself looking right at your own greater self.

Who are you? In Gurdjieff's understanding, you are a knower. You seek and acquire knowledge through your senses. You are the subject, and you constantly focus your mind's attention toward a particular object. This is the act of perception—you the perceiver focusing your attention on that which is being perceived.

Usually your awareness includes only that which you are focused on. You're aware of the known—the perceptual inputs from an outside reality that you are getting to know better through your perception. When you're aware of your breathing, for example, you're getting to know your breathing by focusing your attention on that sensory phenomenon. Much of traditional meditation is contained in this act of holding your mind's full "undivided" attention on an external or internal object or happening, be it your breathing, your thought flows, your whole-body presence, these words, a candle, or a sunset.

Gurdjieff challenges you to employ only part of your attention in being conscious of what you're focusing on and to employ the other part toward being conscious in exactly the other direction—to focus on the knower . . . on yourself.

This might sound so obvious as to be banal. As Robert Earl Burton puts it, "In my long working with this system, one of the strangest observations has been that one has to be taught to remember oneself—it seems so obvious. But how often does one remember oneself during the day?" The act of turning part of your attention inward to your own source seems so simple, and yet for a myriad of reasons we hesitate, or are afraid, or forget to look inward.

Can you turn your mind's attention directly toward the God within? Do you remain aware of yourself as you go about your day? Are you able right now to look inward to the source of your awareness and focus on your own true self—or is there some built-in system that keeps you from doing that?

If there is such an impediment, where did it come from? Is it valid? How might you move beyond the inhibition to where you could look yourself spiritually in the face and remember yourself?

Pause and Experience

This seems like a very good time to pause . . . to focus your attention on your breathing experience . . . and at the same time to look inward with part of your attention . . . and by looking directly to your source of awareness, remember who you really are . . . look with this "divided attention" and observe in action your own mind looking . . . and expand your awareness to include both the observed and the observer . . . at once . . .

Revealing the Knower

A spiritual teacher named Osho, once named Bhagwan Rajneesh, often taught and wrote brilliantly about self-remembering. In *The Book of Secrets,* he says:

> All the techniques of meditation are to reveal the knower. Don't forget yourself and get lost in the object. Remember the subject . . . and then a miracle will happen: as you become aware of both the known and the knower, suddenly you become the third—you become a witness. A witnessing self comes into being. The knower is your mind and the known is the world, and you become a third point, a consciousness, a witnessing self.

This notion that you can become a witness of your own life is very important to our meditation program. In the early *Seven Masters* expansions, you learned to shift from being habitually lost in thoughts about the past and the future to tuning in to your present-moment experiences—your breathing, your heartbeat, the sounds and sights around you. You became aware of the known, the object, the world outside you or inside your body, and your thoughts as they flowed through your mind.

Now you are learning, through divided attention, to also be aware of the knower, of the subject, of your perceiving self. And in this very act of becoming aware of both observed and observer at once, a third point comes instantly into being—the expanded, unattached spiritual consciousness that experiences both the known and the knower at the same time, together in the eternal present moment.

What's amazing about this sixth expansion of consciousness is that when you learn to assume the point of view of the witness, you expand your personal awareness into total oneness with a consciousness that is not of your personal mind but in fact utterly transcendent . . . and one with the Greater Consciousness. Many spiritual masters point generally, if a bit vaguely, in this direction. What Gurdjieff did was to specifically identify this ultimate expansion of consciousness, and teach a path leading directly through this expansion process.

Pause and Reflect

Let's take time off here so you can relax your mind . . . tune in to your breathing and heart . . . and reflect on what we've just explored . . . see what insights come effortlessly to you as you contemplate your own capacity to step back enough from the act of perception, to where you are also aware of the perceiver . . . and in that act, become the witness of your experience . . .

Divided Attention

Let's get as pragmatic as we can now. What does it actually feel like, what is the mental experience, of dividing one's attention in two directions, one outer, one inner, at the same time? Here you will find the simplest way to experience for yourself what self-remembering is all about, in a clear-cut perceptual experiment. After I describe it, do it yourself a few times. Then we'll explore it further in the guided meditation at the end of the chapter.

1. Sit quietly and focus your visual attention on something in the room, any object that you can observe comfortably for a few minutes. Just look and take in this perceptual input—it's the "object" of the experiment.

2. While you remain aware of the object that you are getting to know visually, also begin to be aware of the consciousness

that is directing your attention toward that object, and receiving the perceptual information from that object . . . become aware of the observer in the act of observing . . .

3. While you remain aware of the object being observed as well as the awareness that's focusing on the object, expand your awareness to include the greater awareness, the unattached spiritual witness to the object-subject process.

This process of looking inward in order to know who it is who is experiencing everything we encounter is admittedly a subtle expansion of consciousness. It's also one that human beings have been exploring for quite some time. As Gurdjieff wrote in *Views from the Real World:* "Until a man uncovers himself, he cannot see. So remember yourself always and everywhere. Socrates' words, 'Know thyself,' remain clear for all those who seek true knowledge and being."

Jesus said something similar: "Know the truth, and the truth will set you free." As we've been seeing, the truth he was talking about was almost surely the deeper truth that our mental habits determine our experience, and we can learn to step back and witness the deeper spiritual truth of who we are, beyond the duality of our mind's subject-object perception.

Philosophers and perceptual psychologists agree that in our usual way of experiencing the world there can be no object without a subject, and indeed no subject without an object. This is what Patanjali and Lao Tzu taught, and also what Einstein and Heidelberg and others have been realizing—that human experience consists in an ongoing interaction between subject and object, between sensation and perception, between stimulus and response.

Spiritual reality is clearly one expansion of consciousness beyond scientific reality, however, in our ability establish in our own inner experience an expanded consciousness that exists outside and beyond and independently of the subject-object interaction. We can step back and become the witness who observes the interaction of the mind and its surroundings. This is the ultimate aim of meditation—to transcend the inherent polarity of the material space-time continuum and enter into a quality of consciousness that is eternal, unprogrammed, and independent of our biologically determined cognitive minds.

We're right on the apex of discovery here. This is where all meditation leads us when unimpeded by limiting beliefs and expectations. Again, don't take my word for it—the proof's always in the pudding. As Gurdjieff said: "I ask you to believe nothing that you cannot verify for yourself."

Pause and Experience

If you like, you can now let go of all the theory we've just talked about . . . after reading this paragraph, feel free to put the book aside and experience the "witness" process directly . . . first tune in to your breathing . . . expand your awareness to include your heart . . . your whole body, here in this present moment . . . now look across the room to some object and hold your attention enjoyably and without stress on perceiving this object . . . and at the same time expand your awareness to become conscious of who it is who is focusing on the object . . . and expand again so that you can witness your own mind, looking at the object . . .

Waking Up

Each of the seven expansions we're exploring in this book represents a step beyond darkness into more and more light. Progressively, each expansion will take you out of a relative sleep state and into more and more wakefulness. Waking up has probably always been the dominant metaphor of the meditation world—we are asleep and we need to wake up. In the Gospels, Jesus repeatedly admonished his followers to "wake up!" We speak of someone who has fully expanded into total spiritual consciousness as an "awakened master." Buddha's teachings are full of such encouragement as: "He is awake, and finds joy in the stillness of meditation and the sweetness of surrender . . . live in your heart. Seek the highest consciousness. Happy is the house where a man awakes!"

In a very real sense, as long as we're unaware of our "witness" perspective, we're not yet spiritually awake, because we're unconscious of who we really are. We haven't shined the light of awareness to illuminate our own inner being, and so we remain in darkness even while we shine our light of awareness out upon all the world.

What we hope for in a meditative practice is to gradually shed the scales of sleep and wake up to a quality of consciousness in which our spiritual eyes are wide open, seeing the world without judgment or denial or fear, and at the same time seeing our own inner being without judgment or denial or fear.

In *Self-Remembering*, Robert Earl Burton asks: "What does the term self-remembering mean? It means that your dormant self is remembering to be awake." This act of remembering who we really are does not seem to be a programmed reflex of our animal nature. Instead, our adult consciousness, from Gurdjieff's understanding, must choose to take the leap and perform the necessary mental steps in order to shift from slumber into wakefulness.

Burton also points out that "one reason it is difficult to wake up is because we are surrounded by billions of people who are asleep." His comment is not a judgment but rather a simple psychological observation. The large majority of people consider their everyday state of consciousness to be all there is to consciousness.

Of course, everyone is blessed with momentary glimpses of realization, short flashes of a transcendent state of consciousness. Gazing at a sunset, beholding a rainbow in the sky, or making love, we experience a flash of luminescence that lights up our greater being, and indeed, such experiences can provoke a yearning to stay in that more awakened state always. But then we fall back into our programmed behavior and states of awareness in which we are only somewhat conscious of the outside world, of the perceived. We're not choosing to discipline ourselves to remember to be conscious of the perceiver—to witness the entire subject-object phenomenon of human perception from a higher consciousness that is merged with the Universal Witness.

Pause and Reflect

The spiritual teachers say we are mostly asleep. Do you agree? Are you usually asleep spiritually, not conscious of your own inner light of consciousness, as you go about your day? How do you relate to the very notion that you could break through into a more awake state of consciousness?

Spiritual Inertia

Thus far in this book I've been guiding you along the path of no-effort in meditation. We've now come to the point where we need to talk about spiritual inertia and the challenge of overcoming our usually lethargic mental habits of consciousness. Yes, we cannot force awakening. We cannot push with our egos and "make" ourselves awaken to a higher reality. We can only become more aware of the present moment and, through this awareness, wake up.

At the same time it is no accident that at least three great contemporary spiritual teachers, Gurdjieff, Krishnamurti, and Byron Katie, call their spiritual meditation process "the Work." Robert Earl Burton reiterates the theme of work, saying emphatically to his students, "Effort to remember yourself is the chief thing, because without this effort nothing else has any value; it must be the basis for everything."

On the spiritual path we often encounter seeming paradoxes. Making any effort to achieve spiritual awakening is indeed utterly pointless—we can't force consciousness to expand. At the same time, if we're now mostly asleep and caught up in the inertia of limited mental habits, we must make an effort to dispel the inertia of our mental habits and wake up.

I'm sure you've already discovered this to be true. Sometimes when it's time for your daily meditation, you find your mind making up all sorts of excuses to ditch it and not make the mental effort required to discipline your mind and body into performing the beginning steps of the meditative process. Often, if you don't exert a certain amount of discipline, you simply won't meditate at all. Therefore, you must choose to make the effort to overcome your emotional and mental inertia so that you will enter into the meditative flow. Through discipline, you apply just enough mental effort to direct your attention in valuable meditative directions. Then, with your meditation ship launched, you relax and enter into the effortless flow of the experience.

Even after getting into meditation gear, you may find that occasionally your mind begins to slip out of its focused state and drift off into random thoughts and emotions. When this happens, you exert mental effort once again to bring your attention back to where you choose to hold it. It's so easy to slip into relative unconsciousness. If you want to wake up spiritually, to discover who you really are beyond your conditioned ego self, then Robert Earl Burton is absolutely right: "Effort to remember yourself is the chief thing."

My intent with the *Seven Masters* meditation program is to provide you with a structure and a process that appear almost effortless, in that the meditation process follows the logical spiritual expansions of the human mind step by step, toward a more awakened life. But pushing past some initial inertia is still sometimes necessary.

Often the resistance that blocks a move toward meditating is caused by certain beliefs about the goal of meditation. If you think that you must make a gigantic effort to push yourself to some ultimate sudden blast-through into total enlightenment, then naturally you're going to resist making such an effort in that direction.

So let me make it clear again: I'm not teaching you a process for working hard toward a future radical "sudden awakening," as some of the masters have done. Yes, you will have a great many experiences of suddenly waking up during meditation, but my program does not aim to blast you into total nonstop enlightenment.

Except for very early in my meditative explorations, I've never been interested in sudden total enlightenment. It doesn't make sense to me that we could instantly shift from total spiritual unconsciousness to total spiritual blast-off. Instead, in this book we're exploring what Stephen Levine promises in the title of his wonderful book *A Gradual Awakening*. You'll certainly experience remarkable flashes of clarity and expansion along the path. But watch out for your ego's tendency to want to maintain dominance and feel spiritually superior. It takes an ego act of judgment to decide that you've attained enlightenment—and as soon as you make that ego act of judgment, you've by definition just lost that enlightened state.

As the proverb aptly says, "Those who know don't say, and those who say don't know." Humbleness is all-important on the spiritual path, because as soon as you get a blown-up notion of how great you are spiritually, especially in comparison with others, your ego has taken over and you're back where you started.

Better to let go of all such spiritual ego games and instead, exert just enough effort to point your loving attention toward your already awakened inner nature—simply because you love yourself and want to know the truth of who you are. And always remember that you are already here . . . and already whole.

Pause and Reflect

Feel free to take a few moments to pause and reflect on your own feelings about making an effort to meditate . . . to choose to remember who you really are . . . do you feel the yearning inside you to wake up? . . . are you ready to simply look within and see your ultimate Source and Creative Being?

You Are . . . Awareness

Meditation is often defined as the process through which you finally come to know who you really are. Beyond your memories of what you have done, beyond your self-image of who you should be or how you imagine yourself to be, beyond all your ideas and concepts of your personal identity, you begin to simply see the truth of your deeper essence of being.

Stephen Levine points out that "another word for meditation is simply awareness. Meditation is awareness . . . and the basis of the practice is to directly participate in each moment as it occurs with as much awareness and understanding as possible."

Our ego minds will regularly act out their programmed habits of trying to suck us down into the relative unconsciousness of becoming so attached to our thoughts and our actions, our desires and our fears, that we lose our conscious awareness of what's happening—and thus tend to fall asleep spiritually. Only the regular effort of choosing to expand our consciousness to be aware in the present moment saves us from sinking back into sleep.

What we're discovering in this sixth expansion is that, as we continue to exert enough effort to become more and more alert in the present moment, as we "participate in each moment with as much awareness and understanding as possible," we naturally encounter a reality that pops us into a qualitatively new experience: we no longer identify with the subject-object level of life but are aware from the source of consciousness itself.

The key factor that enables us to make this expansion into pure awareness seems to be letting go of all choice, which means all attachment to outcome. We've seen that in earlier expansions we need to choose to look inward and beyond. But once we're in that process of looking, we then need to let go even of that choosing— so that we are simply pure, unattached awareness. This is the state of consciousness that enables us to truly transcend.

We've seen that our egos are grounded in the ongoing process of choosing one thing over another, this over that, deciding what's best and what's to be avoided. As long as we're observing the world around us from this judgmental point of view, we're locked in the relatively unconscious ego state of desire and choice. The last choice we make each meditation session, with the fifth expansion, is to open up and allow spiritual inflow from beyond our ego center to inundate our personal being.

As soon as we make this final positive ego act, based on the desire to merge with God and be overwhelmed by Spirit, we then must just let go and surrender to whatever is happening in the present moment, without in any way trying to manipulate it. Through this final surrender of all choice and ego direction, we gain the capacity to expand our awareness to include the whole at once—inner and outer, stimulus and response. And in so doing we become spontaneous participants in the present moment, while also remaining totally nonattached witnesses to God's perfect creation.

After moving in meditation through the first five expansions, you'll find that the sixth expansion is in fact effortless. After a few weeks of training, the expansion statement "I know who I am" will naturally point your attention equally inward and outward, so that you are witnessing the truth of your own spiritual identity.

"I know who I am." When you hold these words in your mind, you are not declaring that you already know totally who you are. In the process of gradual awakening, we repeat such words in order to point our attention regularly toward the source of such knowing.

On a certain level, you do already know who you are, and meditation is the process through which you wake up more and more to what you already know. Right at this point of expansion you interface directly with the radical realization that you are utterly one with the source of your personal consciousness. You experience that you are always and forever one with God.

The ultimate witness, after all, is God. As the American Indian tradition often reminds us, we are the eyes and ears of the Creator. And as you let go of all choice, all judgment, all desire, and all attachment, the membrane between your personal consciousness and the infinite consciousness becomes so permeable that you experience the blissful state of total oneness with all of life.

After you make the initial effort to turn your awareness toward your breathing, your heart, your whole-body presence, after you let go of judging yourself and the world and open your heart to receive God's inflow of love and guidance, as you then move into the sixth expansion and say "I know who I am," you will find that no effort is required. The act of self-remembering alone tunes in your awareness to who you really are. And that act is performed simply by remembering to say: "I know who I am."

In this positive light, saying the words "I know who I am" becomes your mantra of celebration . . . your verbal recognition of having woken up . . . to your true infinite self.

Remembering Yourself

Before we move into the guided session for self-remembering, I'd like to share with you a set of sayings from the Gurdjieffian tradition that will be a great help as you contemplate the self-remembering process. You might want to pause now or later and spend time reflecting on each one.

- Meditation is founded upon exploring a total understanding of yourself—a direct seeing of who you are in the present moment, without images and experiences and ideas getting in the way.

- Remember that you are what observes, not what you observe.

- There is no greater miracle than being conscious in this present moment. Everything begins and ends with this.

- Self-remembering is an eighteen-hour-a-day endeavor. You cannot understand self-remembering in thirty minutes. You will want to live with the process every moment of the day.

- The ability of human beings to look within and remember directly who they are is the great mystery of organic life on earth.

- You cannot be present at your destination if you're not present en route. So do everything you can to be present—now.

- Life is real only when you are. And you are real only when you are awake to your own inner presence.

- Try not to twist the present into something it is not. Surrender to it, experience it, and accept it on its own irrefutable terms.

- We are neither the perceived nor the perceiver—we are the witness that experiences the perception. Self-remembering is not a sensation. William Blake said, "I look through my eyes, not with them."

- Have a look at your watching, your witnessing. It is unlimited. It has no beginning, it has no end . . . it is formless, eternal, infinite . . . it is you.

- In the end nothing stands between you and self-remembering but yourself.

SELF-REMEMBERING: GUIDED MEDITATION 6

Make sure you're comfortable, sitting however you choose . . . make whatever movements you want to . . . and gently turn your attention to the air flowing in and out of your nose or mouth . . . expand your awareness to include the movements in your chest and belly as you breathe . . . say to yourself, "I'm breathing freely . . ."

Also, at the same time, be aware of your heart, right in the middle of your breathing . . . be aware of your whole body, here in this present moment . . . your feet . . . your hands . . . your face . . . your whole being . . . be aware of the sounds around you . . . and now say to yourself, "My mind is quiet . . ."

Expand your awareness to include the world around you . . . the room you're in . . . the building you're in . . . the people in your family . . . in your community . . . the people you work with . . . the people driving the highways . . . everyone and everything they're doing right now . . . the world just as it is in this moment . . . God's perfect creation . . . and say to yourself, "I accept the world just as it is . . ."

And as you now hold your attention to your heart, notice how you feel toward your own self . . . observe whether you feel light or heavy in your heart . . . contracted or expansive . . . if you're judging yourself, let the judgments go . . . forgive yourself for everything that needs forgiving . . . just let the love flow . . . and say to yourself, "I love myself just as I am . . ."

Be aware of your breathing . . . your heart . . . your whole-body presence . . . and begin to be aware of where your personal bubble of awareness meets the loving presence of God . . . tune in to whatever emotional upsets and wounds you feel today . . . just let them be there . . . and open your heart as you say a few times, "My heart is open . . . to receive . . . God's healing help . . ."

You're aware of your breathing . . . of all the various sensations coming to you right now from outside your body and from inside . . . you're aware of the outside world . . . at the same time, with part of your awareness, look in the opposite direction, inward . . . to the source of your awareness . . . without any effort, simply be aware of what you're perceiving moment to moment, and at the same time, who is doing the perceiving . . .

If you want, you can gently allow your eyes to open . . . stay with your breathing . . . and observe the room around you while also being aware of who's doing the observing . . .

Now find an object across the room to look at for a few moments . . . stay with your breathing . . . observe the object in the room . . . and at the same time, look inward to the source of your awareness . . . be aware of who's looking at the object, at the same time that you're aware of the object . . .

And as you look inward to your own inner core of being, say to yourself a few times, "I know who I am . . ."

As you continue looking around the room . . . as you continue listening to the sounds around you . . . as you continue experiencing your breathing and all the other sensory happenings . . . also be aware that the awareness of the universe is looking through your eyes . . . you are the eyes and ears of God . . . you are a pure awareness that exists beyond your physical perception system . . . you are the witness . . .

Look . . . and remember who you are . . . look . . . and see . . . "I know who I am . . ."

Let your meditation deepen . . .

FOR INSTANT STREAMED-AUDIO GUIDANCE, PLEASE GO TO
www.7masters.com

CHAPTER 7

Experiencing Bliss—Krishnamurti

Ibegan this book speaking of the spontaneous meditative path of my grandfather and the teachings of another wise man of the Ojai Valley. It seems fitting to now end our exploration of meditation where we began, by tuning in to the utter simplicity and yet radical expansiveness of this wise man's vision of meditation and the spiritual quest.

Krishnamurti was without question the most radical meditation teacher I ever encountered—because he refused to teach any particular meditation method. Instead, he presented the psychological and spiritual parameters of the meditation experience in such a way that we would discover for ourselves how our own minds enter into a meditative state.

Krishnamurti's goal was to encourage his students to open up their hearts and minds to a lifelong inquiry into what it means to be conscious in the present moment. In all his teachings he continually pointed toward the utter simplicity of the spiritual path once we put aside the confusing clutter of the judging mind. He was a teacher who used words to direct his students beyond words—toward the ineffable yet utterly obvious process of looking directly for oneself and seeing to the heart of the matter.

As a result of his focus on the simplicity of spiritual awakening and on the discipline required to attain that simplicity, some people found Krishnamurti a bit frustrating, intellectually obtuse, even downright stubborn at times. He upset many religious folk with his insistence on putting aside all beliefs in order to encounter the true divinity in life. But he stuck to his guns for a lifetime, teaching what he knew to be the truth to those who had ears to hear—and in the end there were a great many who flocked to his gatherings in America, Europe, and India.

He staunchly refused to allow his followers to turn him into a hip guru or spiritual master, even though he talked from the natural posture of an awakened human being. On his deathbed at the ripe age of ninety-two, he uttered these memorable words: "Please now, forget the teacher . . . remember the teachings." Nonetheless, many of us still hold our memory of this man in the highest spiritual regard.

Unwilling Messiah

Who was this man whom hundreds of thousands of people, probably millions, consider the highest spiritual teacher of contemporary times? As a young child in India during the first decade of the twentieth century, he was identified as the living vehicle for the incarnation of the next world messiah, destined to lead all human beings into a radical new spiritual era of peace and awakening. With this fervent anticipation, leaders of the Theosophy movement removed him from his family home in India and summarily adopted him. During the first quarter of the twentieth century, Krishnamurti and his brother were plunged headlong into European and then American cultural life and education, whether they liked it or not.

A quiet, very handsome, sometimes withdrawn boy, Krishnamurti went along with the general life being offered him, yet he remained silent about his own feelings concerning his spiritual identity, and steadfastly refused to enter into serious study of the ancient teachings of the world religious tradition. Finally, as a young man ultimately unwilling to play the messiah role thrust upon him, he publicly threw off the imposed identity of world savior, insisting instead that he was just a man like all others. His only special quality, he insisted, was that he was radically determined to inquire with great passion and total honesty into the ultimate truth of consciousness and human existence.

Because I was born and raised in the same valley where Krishnamurti spent six months a year throughout most of his adult life, from a very early age I often heard the sound of his English-accented voice talking quietly or with rising passion both in small gatherings and in his formal talks in the oak groves of Ojai. Sometimes he would speak to his audience in a quiet loving tone, sometimes with more passion, sometimes even somewhat impatiently as he struggled to find the right words that would move his listeners to realize who they really were, how their minds really worked, and what the meditative process was actually all about.

Often at these public gatherings the scent of the Ojai air would be heady, the temperature ideal, the ambiance quiet and subdued. When I was very young, there were perhaps fifty to a hundred people at the Ojai Krishnamurti talks, but the numbers steadily grew over the years. He would begin a talk by sitting quietly on his straight-back chair in front of the group, waiting for however long it took people to calm down and focus. He would close his eyes and tune in to the present moment with utter concentration, then look out over the audience sitting around him on pads and blankets, encounter them intensely, and finally, in the silence, he would say, with great passion, words such as these:

> I want to ask you today—can you look at yourself without the eyes of the past? Can you watch yourself in action, which is in

relationship, without any movement of thought? When there is no past, there is the bliss of the present moment. Can you put aside all thoughts, quiet your mind, and look to see the truth of this present moment—and thereby directly know yourself?

Most of the people who came to listen to Krishnamurti certainly wanted to leap into this deeply awakened state of mind and heart. And surely some did. But judging from the questions and comments that arose toward the end of the talk, a lot of them didn't seem to be able to let go and make such a leap. Even though he could express his vision of spiritual awakening clearly and emphatically, the actual process eluded many of his listeners.

For his part, Krishnamurti emphatically refused to teach any concrete meditative method to help his followers meet his spiritual challenge. Indeed, he was downright impatient with and critical of all established meditative techniques, the popular gurus, and the meditative teachings of the various world religions. He considered all past teachings and methods a hindrance to spiritual awakening. Instead, he insisted that we discard cultural conditioning, forget what we think we know from past experience, and look directly in the present moment to see how our minds work and who we really are.

"True meditation," he would explain, "is a way of putting aside altogether everything that man has conceived of himself and of the world. In this way, he discovers a totally different kind of mind."

When Krishnamurti was asked specifically about meditation, he would usually reply with concise and yet at the same time mysterious words such as: "Meditation means awareness, both of the world and of the whole movement of oneself. Meditation is to see exactly what is, without any choice, without any distortion, without any thought."

Much as my own children now seem to take for granted the spiritual challenges and insights I struggled so hard to understand in my earlier years, as a child I remember taking in what Krishnamurti was saying mostly by osmosis. I took for granted that what he was talking about was true. He would say to his Ojai audience, "Look at that tree ... let go of your thoughts about it—just see it!" And I'd do what he suggested, never realizing that most of the adults around me found it deucedly difficult to see the tree without getting lost in thoughts about the tree.

In His Presence

A number of times while growing up I had occasion to be in the same space with Krishnamurti at informal local gatherings and a few times up at his home in the orange groves east of town. To be honest, I was more impressed by his friendliness toward a little boy than by his erudite adult conversations. He was around fifty when I was ten. I'd been told that he'd never had children of his own, nor even been married, but he seemed happily at ease with children. A couple of times he preferred to go out and feed the chickens and the milk cow with us rather than continue talking seriously with the older folk. When I think of him now, I often remember the easy joy in his eyes when we were outside just goofing around.

Because we had sporadically encountered each other in Ojai as I was growing up, he knew me by name in later years when I met him in Europe. He seemed to be a mostly solitary fellow, although toward the end of his life it was revealed that he had lived intimately with a deep friend and sexual partner for over twenty years. This seemed to upset some of his followers who assumed he was celibate. Sometimes he was also criticized for expressing impatience with certain of his followers who seemed to hang on his every word, lecture after lecture, without really taking the spiritual plunge he was encouraging. Obviously, he had his own share of emotional challenges. He'd suffered through a difficult, lonely childhood, and sometimes even late in his life he seemed sad and vulnerable to all-too-human upsets. Ultimately, he was a vast complex human mystery, as are we all.

Whatever was happening in his private life, in his public life as a spiritual teacher he remained a fireball of radical ideas and constant challenges. He was certain that each and every one of us had the inherent inner power to experience vast realms of consciousness beyond the confines of our habitual attitudes, judgments, assumptions, and apprehensions about what life is all about.

I had some opportunities as an adult to talk with him privately. He helped me several times by listening to and commenting on my fervent questions about what to do with my life. His insights always jolted me, making me look at my underlying assumptions that were causing my upset and confusion.

One year I decided to move back to Ojai and see whether I could sink new roots in the valley after spending many years elsewhere. I lived just a quarter-mile from Krishnamurti's home and saw him a number of times. He liked to take a daily walk that went past my house, and I would wait for him to come by so that I could walk with him. On warm sunny days other people were usually with him, but on blustery days we walked mostly alone and would go for fifteen or twenty minutes not saying anything at all.

Now that he's gone, I still feel his presence quite often. Especially as I've been writing this book, I've drawn on his subtle guidance just as I draw on my grandfather's guidance, and on the guidance of the other six masters. The truth is, each and every one of us is surely in the loving hands of all the awakened beings, if only we remember to open up and tune in.

Seeing What Is

Krishnamurti was a steadfast advocate of the necessity of a quiet mind in meditation and spiritual exploration. We've been learning his basic guidance in this regard, such as the dedicated observation of our breathing and whole-body presence that leads naturally to quieting the mind. As he regularly would tell his followers, "In order to observe actually what is, in oneself and in the world, a quiet, very still mind is necessary."

Krishnamurti taught quite clearly that the act of focusing on present-moment sensations serves very effectively to quiet the mind. In his words: "If you observe passionately, with intensity, the mind inevitably becomes quiet." He likewise considered the primary shift we've been learning, from the cognitive mode into the perceptual mode, to be the gateway into realms of consciousness that the thinking mind can't even imagine: "Meditation is the seeing of what is, the looking and the listening, and the going beyond it—this is what takes place when the brain, the mind, and the body are really quiet and harmonious—when the mind, the body, and the heart are completely one. Then you live a totally different kind of life."

Like many other spiritual teachers, Krishnamurti placed great emphasis on learning how to watch one's own thoughts going by and thus observing the thinking mind in action. His guidance included not only watching the thoughts as they arise one after the other but seeing at once, in a flash, the entire programmed contents of the mind: "One must find a way of observing the mind without analysis—a way of observing the whole content of consciousness without the analyzer."

Over and over again, in many different variations, he would ask: "What is the nature, the structure of that inner judge who is watching? That observer is the past—the past knowledge and ideas you have stored up. Thought is the response of the past. So thought is never free. It is always old."

Krishnamurti brought to his listeners that special spark of realization that moves beyond idea and into action. He was constantly admonishing people not to take his word for what he was saying but rather to look directly to their own immediate experience to find out what is true. He insisted that he not be treated as a guru or a master who knew everything already—he wanted to be seen instead as a provocateur who pushed people to discover reality for themselves.

"Realize by direct looking," he would say, "that there is no division between the observer and the observed, between the thinker and the thought. Then you see—then you observe what actually is. And when you see actually what is, you are already beyond it."

Like the Zen teachers, Krishnamurti insisted that it is utterly futile to seek anything or to cling to beliefs or to hunger for a particular experience, however grand it might be spiritually. In his words:

> The mind must be totally free of the demand for experience and the search for truth. Completely end all seeking. Have no beliefs whatsoever, don't be committed to any religion, have no authority whatsoever. Be entirely free of any form of belief, any form of fear. . . . When inquiring into such an extraordinary question, there must be the freedom of actually not knowing a thing about it. Be free of conditioning, so that your mind is free to observe. . . . One must have this freedom from all belief, from all commitments, so that one is committed to the whole of life, not to one fragment of it. Commit your whole being, your whole energy, vitality, and passion, to the entirety of life. Then we can proceed to find out what it means to meditate.

Radical Freedom

Krishnamurti was a fanatic about inner freedom. At one point, when asked about how to control the thoughts of the mind so as to attain freedom from the past, he said:

> Freedom is at the beginning of meditation, not the end. What is important from beginning to end is not controlling thought,

but understanding it, understanding the origin, the beginning of thought, which is in yourself. Thought springs from the storehouse of memory. Simply look, and see—then you are already free. In meditation one has to find out whether there is an end to knowledge. There is freedom only when there is freedom from the known.

Psychologists and philosophers often tried to undermine Krishnamurti's logic at his lectures, insisting that pragmatically we can never be free from the known, that we are at heart conditioned animals whose every act is a result of past conditioning. Krishnamurti would abide no such efforts to use deductive rationality to divert us from looking into the heart of the matter. He would counter without hesitation: "The real issue is, can thought function when necessary, and then be completely still at other times? The mind has to find out whether the brain cells can be totally quiet, and thus respond to a dimension they do not know."

This insistence that the mind can be quiet and at the same time exceedingly sensitive and aware and responsive lies at the heart of Krishnamurti's understanding of psychological and spiritual liberation. "You must have a very quiet mind," he would insist, "because only then can you see. If you are chattering, if your mind is constantly in movement, rushing all over the place, obviously it cannot look, it cannot listen totally."

A primary theme throughout Krishnamurti's lifetime was that the mind either functions in a fragmented way—as a result of an unrelenting stream of judgmental thoughts and concepts that divide reality into categories—or it functions as a whole, utterly silent yet with total awareness, wisdom, and spontaneous response to the world each and every moment. "See the necessity," he often said, "of having this delicate, subtle mind which is absolutely quiet. It is only such a mind that sees the whole of life as a unitary movement, not fragmented. Such a mind acts totally, not fragmentarily, because it acts out of complete stillness."

He knew from his own experience that the mind can be absolutely quiet, and that indeed in most instances we do best to keep the thinking mind entirely silent so that we can perceive rather than conceive. In his words, "It is the direct perception of 'what is' that brings about a radical change. In a quiet mind there is a movement that is totally different—that is of a different dimension, of a different quality."

Krishnamurti taught that what awakens the true potential of human consciousness is the very act of looking, of listening, of perceiving what is happening around us and within us in the present moment.

> You must begin at the beginning, and the first step is the last step in meditation—uncondition the mind by becoming aware, by becoming totally attentive. . . . Allow that mountain, that tree, to absorb you completely. Give attention, passionately, intensely, look and listen completely—and to listen and see completely, your mind must be quiet. This is meditation. When you understand what quietness is, when you understand beauty, understand love, see how your mind works, and who you are . . . then out of that direct seeing comes an extraordinarily quiet mind.

Krishnamurti taught that when we quiet our thoughts, we see with the whole mind. By shifting from cognitive fixations to perceptions in the present moment, we come into a unified experience. "The act of seeing is the only truth; there is nothing else. Look at the tree . . . see it completely with the totality of your mind and heart, not a fragment of it."

Through our immersion in this direct seeing and our choice to live in the meditative moment, we enter naturally into the infinite realms of consciousness—where we discover bliss. "There is a vast expanse of the mind which usually we never touch or know. That mind is immeasurable. We don't know the quality of it because we have never looked at anything completely, with the totality of our mind, of our heart, of our nerves, of our eyes, of our ears. For this there is no method. You must simply make the whole field completely sensitive. In that lies the only true revolution."

It's so simple, yet so utterly sublime. "All one has to do is to see. And this seeing is the act of love. Seeing destroys all barriers. Seeing brings us intimately in contact with life. . . . What is important is not to learn but to see, and to listen. And out of this seeing and listening you will find that all separation between the observer and the observed comes to an end."

And what happens when, through perceptual awakening, all separation comes to an end? "If you can see, you have nothing else to do. The mind has emptied itself of all its content, of every suggestion, every probability, every possibility. The mind is completely active—and empty. . . . Then there is a tremendous revolution, your whole action undergoes a radical change. You are completely whole."

Let's take a few moments here to pause and allow the wave of Krishnamurti's words to flow over us . . . as we bring our mind's attention fully into the present moment . . . breathing . . . listening . . . seeing . . . being . . .

The Bliss Factor

Many "serious" spiritual teachers shy away from talking about how meditation can make us feel good. Some of them consider it overly mundane, even selfish and hedonistic, to have as one of our main motivations for meditating the intention of shifting our general mood from upset, worried, agitated, dull, and depressed to joyful, bright, passionate, and, yes, even downright blissful.

Meditation is a primary inner tool for transforming banged-around emotional and psychic systems into bright beacons of compassion, pleasure, clarity, and good old-fashioned fun. The "laughing Buddha" has been a primary inspiration in this regard. Alan Watts, for all his human foibles and intellectual genius, was regularly attuned to what he called the "convolutions of the great guffaw" as he brought his listeners to see the ultimately humorous nature of spiritual exploration, and our responsibility to merge meditative devotion with joy, humor, and bliss. Likewise, oldtime Sufi teachers such as Sam Lewis were often caught up in laughter, ecstasy, fun, and frolic. Perhaps their defining quality wasn't seriousness in the face of the divine, but an outflowing of passionate joy at just being alive and conscious on this planet.

The spontaneous experience of bliss has also surfaced regularly in most religious traditions. Many saints of the Catholic Church found themselves transported into mystic bliss, as did followers of Buddha. Bliss has usually been regarded as a pure gift of grace that comes to people unexpectedly, exploding inside them and then leaving. Indeed, this experience is not something we can selfishly decide to generate and then perform certain rituals to make it appear in our lives. The experience seems to fall upon us out of the blue.

What, then, is this thing called bliss, and how can we encourage its presence in our everyday lives? Bliss is perhaps more easily defined by what it is not. It is not fear. It is not dread. Bliss comes into being only in the absence of anxiety. Furthermore, it is not anger or judgment or rejection or denial. Bliss is not anything negative.

Bliss thrives in the presence of love, compassion, acceptance, trust, and all things positive. Bliss is the flow of pure Spirit into our lives. It is our natural state when we let go of all our thoughts and judgments and contractions and beliefs and other cognitive baggage and simply open up to the passion of being alive and filled with our ultimate life source, God's infinite creative joy and love.

It may be a psychological truth that when there is zero fear in a person's mind, there is an abundance of joy. Likewise, as

Krishnamurti says, "When there is no past, there is the bliss of the present moment." As long as we hold our focus fully in the perceptual realms of consciousness and act to quiet the mind's past-based associations and thoughts, we quite predictably awaken the natural experience of bliss in the present moment.

If we design our daily meditation so that we progressively expand beyond our busy thoughts, relax, and let go of the future and all its worries, opening our hearts to the inflow of love and healing grace, we naturally arrive at a point in our meditation where we feel fully alive in the present moment, with love and joy inflowing . . . and bliss abiding.

As Krishnamurti describes it: "In that act of seeing, there is all beauty. And with beauty there is love—and when there is love, you have nothing more to do. Where you are, you have bliss, you have heaven."

Giving Yourself Permission

Even though bliss is always ready to come flowing into our lives, God or the Tao or whatever you call the Infinite Creator doesn't over push. We must give ourselves permission to feel good and open our hearts to the inflow of good feelings, if we want to receive them. To receive the uplifting joy of spiritual awakening, we must let down all our ego defenses and open up in total trust.

But such total yielding to overwhelming passion and uncontrolled feelings and experiences has traditionally been associated with unacceptable emotional and sexual abandonment and all sorts of other supposed crimes of passion. As I've written at length in *Sex and Spirit*, our ingrained fears about feeling good and surrendering to pleasure directly block not only sexual but spiritual awakening. Many of us are seriously armored against ever being overwhelmed by passion and ecstasy—we expect terrible things to happen to us if we lose ego control.

Bliss and passion lie on an energetic continuum. Bliss is the passive dimension, and passion the active dimension, of the same inflow of good feelings from beyond our personal bubble of identity. In both cases, we're inundated with an energy that fills us, inspires us, and makes us feel wonderful and at one with the cosmos.

During your next meditation session, when you come to this seventh expansion, at first just watch what happens in your mind when you say the focus statement: "I am here ... now ... in bliss." Observe without judgment the thoughts that spring into action and the images that come to mind when you consider surrendering to passion and the flow of good feelings into your heart and body. In the process of catching possible anti-bliss reactions in action, you'll become aware of your conditioning related to bliss, and step by step you'll let go of it.

Krishnamurti pointed out over and over again that being filled with a charge of passion to know the truth is the essential ingredient needed for looking directly and seeing clearly who we really are. Passion is the positive, inspired energy that moves human beings—and when we come to perceive our human nature directly, our passion is naturally transformed into ... bliss.

This is the journey we are walking together here day by day, expansion by expansion, as we tap our deeper core of consciousness through observing each new moment in action. We tend to begin each meditation session fully engaged in all our everyday emotional worries and ego games. We then move through all seven expansions of consciousness that encourage a new awakening of our spirit in the present moment. In the process we transform who we are, over and over again, as we learn to merge our personal souls with the Infinite Reality. And regularly, through tapping the energy released during meditation, we experience the bliss that is at the center of our being.

Krishnamurti saw this meditative process of regularly opening to passionate energy and inspired realization as the act of transformation that our society so desperately needs right now:

Unless there is deep psychological revolution, mere reformation on the periphery will have little effect. The psychological revolution, which I think is the only revolution, is possible through meditation. That revolution can only take place at the very center of our being and requires a great abundance of energy. Meditation is the release of that total energy.

EXPERIENCING BLISS: Guided Meditation 7

We now come to the last of our seven guided meditations. You'll notice that this final meditation includes all seven expansions and represents the whole flow of the *Seven Masters* meditation program. While memorizing and mastering the program, you can turn to this script whenever you want to move through the full seven-expansion meditation.

Each of the paragraphs in this expansion represents a compact version of one of the earlier expansions, and guides you immediately in the direction of the focus phrase. You'll find that, after a couple of weeks of being guided through this primary process, you'll have naturally memorized the general flow, and only need to remember to say each focus phrase in order to enter into one after another of the meditations . . . enjoy!

And so, make sure you're comfortable, sitting however you choose . . . feel free to make whatever movements you want to . . . and gently turn your attention to the air flowing in and out of your nose or mouth . . . expand your awareness to include the movements in your chest and belly as you breathe . . . and say to yourself, "I'm breathing freely . . ."

Expand your awareness to include your heart, beating right in the middle of your breathing . . . be aware of your whole body, here in this present moment . . . your feet . . . your hands . . .

your face ... your whole being ... be aware of the sounds around you ... and now say to yourself, "My mind is quiet ..."

Expand your bubble of awareness to include the world around you ... the people in your family ... in your community ... the people you work with ... everyone and everything they're doing right now ... the world just as it is in this moment ... God's perfect creation ... and say to yourself, "I accept the world, just as it is ..."

And as you now hold your attention to your heart, notice how you feel toward your own self ... observe whether you feel light or heavy in your heart ... contracted or expansive ... if you're judging yourself, just let the judgments go ... forgive yourself for everything that needs forgiving ... just let the love flow ... and say to yourself, "I love myself, just as I am ..."

Be aware of your breathing ... your heart ... your whole-body presence ... and begin to be aware of where your personal bubble of awareness meets the infinite loving presence of God ... tune in to the emotional upsets and wounds that you feel today ... just let them be there ... and surrender to spiritual guidance as you say a few times, "My heart is open ... to receive ... God's healing help ..."

You're aware of your breathing ... of all the various sensations coming to you right now from outside your body, and from inside ... as you stay aware of your perceptions from the outside world, at the same time, look with part of your awareness in the opposite direction, inward to the source of your awareness ... without any effort, simply be aware of what you're perceiving moment to moment and, at the same time, who is doing the perceiving ... and as you look inward and become one with your own inner core of being, say to yourself a few times, "I know who I am . . ."

Allow your breaths to come and go on their own . . . listen to the sounds around you . . . pay full attention to what is happening right now . . . experience all at once . . . pure awareness . . . of the whole . . . let thoughts fall away . . . memories fall away . . . desires fall away . . . give yourself permission to be totally free, to experience what actually is . . . this . . . here . . . now . . . experience the movement of life . . . be totally attentive . . . extraordinarily quiet . . . completely sensitive . . . whole . . . and loving . . .

When there is love, there is nothing more to do . . . where you are, you have bliss . . . be open to a new experience as you say "I am here . . . now . . . in bliss . . ."

As the music plays, allow your meditation to deepen . . .

FOR INSTANT STREAMED-AUDIO GUIDANCE, PLEASE GO TO
www.7masters.com

Final Words

Your Daily Meditation Program

You now know the full flow of the seven expansions that make up the *Seven Masters* meditation program. You have the transformation tools in hand. Nothing stands between you and a lifetime of inner exploration, realization, and bliss. Let me list again the seven core sayings that turn your attention immediately in directions that awaken your experience of your deeper being. Do you know each of these expansions fairly well already? Do they stimulate a response and a movement inside you?

"I'm breathing freely."

"My mind is quiet."

"I accept the world just as it is."

"I love myself just as I am."

"My heart is open to receive."

"I know who I am."

"I am . . . here . . . now . . . in bliss."

What to Do Now

All too often we read quickly through a spiritually inspiring book, become hopeful that we can truly transform our lives in beautiful directions—but then as soon as we finish with the book our passion begins to dissipate. Our universal tendency is to close one book and immediately look for another. My intent with this new approach to meditation instruction is to make sure you move successfully beyond the first talk-about stage of written instruction and inspiration, into the deeper and vastly more rewarding second stage of regular direct experience through a daily spiritual practice.

As you now approach the end of this flow of words, I encourage you to take time to clarify in your mind a daily meditative game plan that will enable you to advance steadily on the spiritual path into more and more fulfilling experiences and realizations. Toward this aim, my colleagues and I have developed a number of meditation-support systems that will guide you successfully through the next phases of your journey.

For some of you, of course, this book will be all you need, and after only one reading you will have internalized the entire process. If this is true, wonderful! If not, here are some other options to explore, after you've read through the book and picked up a beginning sense of your own inner meditative potential.

These programs have been specifically designed to augment and expand on the *Seven Masters, One Path* text. Not only will they serve you well as a lifelong resource and support system but they also provide access to a meditative community of like-minded people learning and exploring the same program and spiritual process that you're involved in. This sense of shared experience can prove of vital importance in your spiritual life.

The Four Meditation Time Frames

Even as you're first beginning to memorize and internalize the meditation process, you'll want to regularly practice the *Seven Masters* meditation each day, or several times a day. These four time-frame structures offer you a full range of possibilities for integrating meditation into your daily schedule. At first you'll probably want to employ either the written or audio-guidance for moving through the seven expansions. Soon you'll find that you don't need the external support in your meditations.

HALF-HOUR DAILY MEDITATION

Ideally you will set aside half an hour each day, preferably at the same time and place, to be guided through or to guide yourself through the full *Seven Masters* meditation process. In a half-hour practice, you spend three minutes more with each expansion (around twenty focused breaths per expansion). After you've done the seventh expansion, you can quietly meditate without further guidance and open yourself to a new experience each time. A formal audio-guidance program for this half-hour time frame is available online at www.7masters.com.

Of course, you can meditate for longer than half an hour whenever you want to. Also, you can do this meditation more than once a day if time permits. And a particular theme seems especially important, feel free to focus just on that meditation for an entire session that day. What's important is to make sure that each and every day you pause and focus within, so as to establish a lifelong habit of dedicating at least some time to your spiritual adventure.

TEN-MINUTE MEDITATION

Along with your main meditation—or perhaps as your main meditation—you will also find a short-form ten-minute meditation routine to be of great benefit and pleasure one or more times a day. In the ten-minute time frame you devote six breaths per expansion, saying each focus phrase one or two times with the first couple of breaths, and then being silent for the next few breaths before moving on to the next expansion. After the seventh expansion, you can simply "be in bliss" for however long you want, or you can return to the beginning and focus on the expansion that most attracts you right then. At our website you'll find an audio-guidance program specifically for this time frame.

TWO-MINUTE MEDITATION

Whenever you have just a couple of minutes free, I highly encourage you to pause and simply say each of the seven focus phrases, one after the other. Devote one or two breaths to each of the sayings, focusing your full attention on each of the expansions for a short but invaluable time. You'll find that the more you experience each expansion in longer-format meditations, the deeper and faster you'll be able to move your attention during the short-format meditations. It's quite remarkable how we can learn to move rapidly into deep meditation after only a bit of practice and repeat experience. In just two minutes you can rapidly expand your consciousness beyond your habitual mental patterns and into a more conscious, loving, spiritual stance in whatever you're doing. In so doing, you will bring into your environment a bright clear compassionate light that everyone around you will benefit from.

MINI-MEDITATION

When you don't even have two minutes, you'll find that just thirty seconds of meditation a few times a day can transform your experience of life. If you simply pause long enough to remember to be aware of your breathing and say, "I'm breathing freely," this quick expansion into full breath awareness will awaken your whole-body consciousness. As we explored in chapter 1, you transform your day when you're aware of your breathing. It doesn't matter what you're doing or who you're with. And no one need know what you're up to . . . just take thirty seconds to tune in to your breathing, and your heart . . . and you'll awaken your entire being to the power and pleasure of the present moment.

Pause and Reflect

You might want to pause for a few moments, put the book aside, tune in to your breathing . . . and contemplate how you feel about dedicating at least one or more time periods each day of the rest of your life to bringing a higher consciousness into your everyday routines . . . look to your heart . . . do you truly yearn to be a more spiritual being? . . . are you ready to discipline yourself the minimal amount required to master a daily meditation practice?

Online Community and Meditation Support

The process of learning how to meditate is different for each person. You will inevitably have your own particular meditation needs, focusing difficulties, emotional challenges, and mental blocks that might arise. They may be minor or major, and they may appear tomorrow or next month or two years down the road. The intention of the following training programs and community support systems is to make sure that wherever you are in the mastery of a meditation practice, you can find the tools and help you need to succeed with your goal, and tap your spiritual depths on a daily basis.

Until the advent of the Internet, we were seriously limited in our student-teacher interactions to either the printed format in books and workbooks, or in-person lectures and seminars in your region. Now we are able to meet anytime, anywhere, through online interaction, and the mastery process has thus been greatly accelerated. The use of inexpensive CD programming also lets you access my voice wherever you might be, whenever you want.

The following programs, available at www.7masters.com, are designed to meet the various challenges that I've seen arise as people begin to develop a successful meditation practice and move through the various stages of spiritual awakening.

THREE-WEEK TRAINING PROGRAM

The first approach to deepening your memorization of and intimate familiarity with each of the seven expansions is to return to the beginning of this book and devote three days to each of the chapters and meditative expansions. Within this formal time structure, and with a commitment to a scheduled learning structure, you will be able to go deeper into each aspect of the seven meditations and truly make them your own.

The total time commitment for this training program is twenty-one days. You'll want to set aside perhaps half an hour to an hour each day to read the chapter you're focusing on and do the meditation in depth. The audio-guidance available on the web or a CD provides a ten-minute focus on each expansion and will further aid you in becoming deeply grounded in each expansion. A visual-calendar structure is also available at www.7masters.com so that you can print out your schedule and thus easily remember what to do each day. This calendar also provides further guidance in following this three-week training program.

ONLINE WORKSHOP AND THEME SEMINARS

My colleagues and I have designed a specially structured learning process that you can access online. In this online workshop, we work together through each of the seven expansions, at a pace of your choosing. You have full freedom to take whatever time you need to make sure you understand each expansion and master the process to the best of your ability. The workshop structure enables you to ask any questions on your mind about your own experience, so that you can advance rapidly and smoothly through the learning process. The online workshop also provides a wealth of additional information and guidance not found elsewhere, as well as an expanded audio-guidance system for optimum effortless learning of the seven expansions. From time to time we also offer "Theme Seminars" on topics related to meditation and personal growth.

QUESTION-ANSWER AND ARTICLE LIBRARY

For each of the *Seven Masters* expansions, we provide a special online forum where you can ask questions related to that theme and I will answer your question with a printed reply. The growing body of discussions about each of the expansions serves as a solid support system when you need quick information and guidance on a particular topic or concern. We also occasionally do a live online forum in which we interact more immediately and get directly to the core of questions together. I'll be posting more and more articles of general interest for your further explorations.

PHONE AND E-MAIL COUNSELING

There are times when direct verbal interaction about a specific meditation concern can rapidly resolve issues that would otherwise block a successful meditation practice. When you've done your best through the other available resources to resolve a meditation dilemma and still feel stuck, I or a colleague will be available for a limited amount of phone consultation. In this live format we can discuss your meditation situation and guide you directly toward a resolution of your dilemma. You'll find more information on this dimension of the *Seven Masters* program at the www.7masters.com website.

REGIONAL WORKSHOPS

I've always highly valued the weekend workshop format for teaching meditation, in an intensive atmosphere where together we go very deeply into our inner experience. With all the Internet opportunities these days, we tend to lose sight of the special value of gathering in person to explore who we are and how we can best use our minds and bodies to awaken our hearts and souls. My commitment is to be available regionally as much as possible, and in-person weekend workshops remain a key aspect of the *Seven Masters* community. If you sign up for our weekly e-mail newsletter, I'll also alert you to related live events in your region that might prove of great value to attend.

CHAT ROOMS AND ONLINE MEDITATION GROUPS

Online chat rooms are a wonderful experience for meditators because you can talk back and forth with people who are busy learning the same process you're learning. By sharing your experiences with other similar-minded folk, you can gain new insights into the meditation process and provide essential friendly support to each other as you move deeper into meditative explorations. When you go to the www.7masters.com website, you'll find several different topics and chat opportunities. You can also start your own group with people who are beginning to master the *Seven Masters* program at the same time you are. This offers you an opportunity to create a long-lasting meditation group that may be valuable in many ways.

Seven Masters
WEEKLY E-MAIL COMMUNITY NEWSLETTER

Along with the inspirational and educational offerings that are regularly updated on the www.7masters.com website, you can also sign up for our free weekly e-mail newsletter to stay effortlessly in touch and receive instant access to new audio-guidance programs and special community happenings. In the weekly newsletter you'll also find new discussions of a host of meditation themes, as well as reviews of the best new books on meditation and spiritual exploration and the best meditation-music and audio-guidance CDs and videos. The newsletter has a regularly updated calendar of related events in your region that might expand your sense of spiritual community and participation. I highly recommend that you go online at www.7masters.com and sign up for the newsletter so that we can regularly be in touch.

In Sum

And so the time comes when the end of this book is just a page or two away, and you'll be taking your unique next steps to master these meditations and make them your own. In ending, let me express very simply what I feel we've learned here together.

We've seen how all seven of our selected spiritual masters have guided their students toward using their own power of attention in special ways, in order to awaken deeper realms of consciousness. All seven masters have shown that our judgmental minds cause our inner suffering, and that a quiet mind leads to inner awakening and peace.

Furthermore, all seven masters have emphasized that only by fully accepting reality just as it is in the present moment, and accepting and loving ourselves just as we are, can we expand into greater levels of spiritual consciousness and clarity. And finally, all seven masters have agreed that we must open our hearts and minds to the wisdom and healing touch of the Greater Consciousness if we want to discover who we really are and our deeper blissful nature.

You now know specific ways in which you can follow the meditative teachings of the world's spiritual masters and have your own personal experience of these seven expansions. You have an online support system that will help you and encourage you whenever you want such help. You also have instant access to a spiritual community where you can make new meditative friends and explore any and all new avenues that open up and appeal to you as your spiritual journey continues.

Let me end with a wonderful ancient Taoist saying that Alan Watts introduced me to. It rounds off our discussion with a perfect symmetry.

ANCIENT TAOIST MEDITATION

I close my eyes
and see clearly . . .

I stop trying to listen
and hear truth . . .

I am silent
and my heart sings . . .

I seek no contact
and find union . . .

I am still
and move forward . . .

I am gentle
and need no strength . . .

I am humble
and remain whole . . .

Meditations at a Glance

Breath Watch
Experience breath sensations in nose . . .
also experience movements in chest and belly . . .
I am breathing freely . . .

Quiet Mind
Observe breathing and heartbeat together . . .
also expand to hear sounds . . .
My mind is quiet . . .

Accepting Truth
Are you at peace . . . or suffering? . . .
stop judging . . . embrace the present situation . . .
I accept the world just as it is . . .

Heart Awakening
Are you judging yourself? . . .
open to inflow of unconditional love . . .
I love myself just as I am . . .

Emotional Healing
Observe and accept emotions . . . have faith . . .
let the feelings heal . . .
My heart is open . . .
to receive . . . God's healing help . . .

Self-Remembering
Listen to sounds . . . see everything at once . . .
look to your inner source of awareness . . .
I know who I am . . .

Experiencing Bliss
Give yourself permission . . .
open up to insight and passion . . .
I am here . . . now . . . in bliss . . .

Support Group Directory

Meditation is very much a solitary experience in which you look inward to your own inner core of being. However, meditating in a group is also universally recognized and practiced as a deep and wonderful process of shared consciousness and focus.

REGIONAL MEDITATION GROUPS

To help you find a meditation group in your area, the *Seven Masters* online support site posts all the listings you send in to us online of local groups that are practicing *Seven Masters* meditation or similar meditations. Please go to www.7masters.com and click on "community" to access a group in your area, or to list your group.

STARTING A NEW GROUP

If you would like to help create a *Seven Masters* meditation group in your area, or meet with people with similar interests to get together and discuss your experiences, please e-mail www.7masters.com with the "contact us" button, and we'll help bring you together with other folks who have read the book and are practicing the meditation.

ONLINE COMMUNITY

We also offer online support groups in which you can join a chat room with people who are beginning to learn the meditations at the same time you are, so that you can share your experiences, discover how other people are exploring the meditation process, and make new friends! It's easy—just go to www.7masters.com.

Online Audio-Guidance

As you've noticed throughout the text of this book, the online audio-guidance dimension of this meditation training system can prove very important. The discussions in this book will help you develop a solid conceptual understanding of the principles and techniques of quieting your mind at will. Some of you will need only the written guidance through the techniques to master the programs.

However, most people run up against an inherent difficulty when working with any meditation training text. Almost all of us have suffered the experience of reading an inspiring book by an able spiritual teacher, but then feeling frustrated in our attempts to master the techniques simply by reading about them. After all, the teacher almost certainly learned the techniques from hearing his own teacher guiding him through the process over and over. And the teacher developed his variations on the ancient meditation themes by guiding his own students through the process over and over—using the spoken voice, not the written word.

For years as a writer of spiritual and psychological texts, I struggled with the question of how to better serve my readers in the learning process. How can you manage to close your eyes, let go of the work of reading, and listen directly to my voice guiding you through the learning process over and over until you truly master the meditation?

It's curious to find high technology providing us with our meditative solution. Now that streamed audio is a reality for everyone on broadband or cable Internet, you can access my voice to guide you through the meditations of this book with just a click of your mouse. This new format for delivering audio-guidance programs so that anyone can instantly access the audio-guidance dimensions of my work is truly exciting: it combines the still-essential written text, which delivers the fundamental concepts needed to understand a new experience, with instant access to the audio-guidance I regularly provide my students and clients.

As you've perhaps already discovered, the script for each chapter's guided meditation appears at the end of the chapter accompanied by the Internet address (www.7masters.com), which takes you immediately to a streamed-audio program where you can listen to my voice guiding you through the meditation process. Thus, whenever you want personal guidance, you can go online, close your eyes, and relax into an intimate experience of the process you are learning.

For those of you who don't have access to a broadband computer or who want to listen to the audio-guidance away from your computer, there is also a low-cost CD version of the audio programs that you can order online at www.7masters.com or by sending $12 (includes shipping and handling) to: *Seven Masters* CD, PO Box 861, Kilauea, HI 96754.

Advanced Programs

The essence of meditation is to keep it as simple as possible. At the same time, after you have done a meditation for a considerable amount of time, you often find that you are ready for a variation on the general theme, or a special application of the meditation program for your particular needs.

Over the years I've developed a number of meditation programs that run parallel to the *Seven Masters* meditations and offer special windows of experience into our deeper spiritual nature. Some of these programs have been recorded; you can go to the www.7masters.com website and listen to them at your leisure, find the one that appeals to you the most right now, and begin to master that new meditation.

I welcome you to this lifelong exploration of your meditative potential. You'll also find psychological healing techniques, based on my *Quiet Your Mind* text and other self-help programs, that will help you explore whether emotional problems are standing in the way of your meditation experience.

Each morning when you wake up, you naturally enter the new day with a particular interest or concern that seems most important to deal with or explore that day. I've structured the online support system at www.johnselby.com to meet you where you find yourself most under pressure at the moment, and to offer a guided session or series of sessions that will provide genuine relief and insight. Feel free to take advantage of these guided programs whenever you like!

Based on online and written feedback to experiences with the *Seven Masters* meditations, I am also developing special programs to meet your needs and expand your meditative experience. Please write and let me know your concerns and interests in future programs.

References

CHAPTER I: BREATH WATCH—PATANJALI

A. H. Almaas, *Being and the Meaning of Life* (Berkeley, CA: Almaas Publishing, 1990).

Sri Aurobindo, *The Adventure of Consciousness* (Pondicherry, India: Sri Aurobindo Trust, 1968).

Joachim-Ernst Berendt, *Nada Brahma: The World of Sound* (Rochester, VT: Destin Books, 1987).

Bernard Bouanchaud, *The Essence of Yoga: A New Translation and Reflections on the Yoga Sutras of Patanjali* (Portland, OR: Rudra Press, 1997).

Ram Dass, *Journey of Awakening: A Meditator's Handbook* (New York: Bantam Books, 1978).

Eknath Easwaran, trans., *The Upanishads* (Tomales, CA: Nilgiri Press, 1987).

Evans-Wentz, W. Y., *Tibetan Yoga and Sacred Doctrines, or Seven Books of Wisdom of the Great Path, According to the Late Lama Kazi Dawa-Samdup* (Oxford: Oxford University Press, 1935, 1958).

Edward Gendlin, *Focusing* (New York: Bantam, 1981).

Hazrat Inayat Khan, *The Mysticism of Sound and Music* (Boston: Shambhala, 1996).

Ann Myren and Dorothy Madison, eds., *Living at the Source: Yoga Teachings of Vivekananda* (Boston: Shambhala, 1993).

Andrew Newberg and Eugene D'Aquili, M.D., *Why God Won't Go Away* (New York: Ballantine, 2001).

Simon Pinker, *How the Mind Works* (New York: W. W. Norton, 1997).

Larry Rosenberg, *Breath by Breath: Insight Meditation* (Boston: Shambhala, 1998).

Rabindranath Tagore, *The Religion of Man* (London: George Allen, 1953).

William Teasdale, *The Mystic Heart: Discovering a Universal Spirituality in the World's Religions* (Novato, CA: New World Library, 1999).

Paramahansa Yogananda, *Autobiogrpahy of a Yogi* (Los Angeles: Self-Realization Fellowship, 1987).

Eckhard Tolle, *The Power of Now: A Guide to Spiritual Enlightenment* (Novato, CA: New World Library, 1999).

S. Yoga Venkatesananda, *Vasistha's Yoga* (Albany: State University of New York Press,1993).

CHAPTER 2: QUIETING THE MIND—LAO TZU

John Austin, *Zen and the Brain: Toward an Understanding of Meditation and Consciousness* (Cambridge, MA: MIT Press, 1998).

Hubert Benoit, *The Supreme Doctrine* (New York: Pantheon, 1955).

John Blofeld, *The Teachings of Huang Po* (New York: Grove Press, 1970).

Thomas Cleary, *The Essential Tao* (New York: HarperCollins, 1991).

Elwood Conze, *Buddhism: Its Essence and Development* (Oxford: Cassirer, 1953).

Eugen Herrigel, *Zen and the Art of Archery* (Baltimore: Penguin, 1960).

Christmas Humphreys, *Zen Buddhism* (London: Heinemann, 1949).

Philip Kapleau, *Three Pillars of Zen* (Boston: Beacon Press, 1968).

Thomas Merton, *Mystics and Zen Masters* (New York: Farrar, Straus and Giroux, 1967).

Stephen Mitchell, ed., *The Enlightened Heart: An Anthology of Sacred Poems* (New York: Harper and Row, 1989).

Andrew Newberg and Eugene D'Aquili, *Why God Won't Go Away: Brain Science and the Biology of Belief* (New York: Ballantine Books, 2001).

D. T. Suzuki, *Essays in Zen Buddhism* (London: Rider, 1951).

Shunryu Suzuki, *Zen Mind, Beginner's Mind: Informal Talks on Meditation and Practice* (New York: Weatherhill, 1970).

Alan Watts, *Still the Mind: An Introduction to Meditation* (Novato, CA: New World Library, 2000).

———. *The Book on the Taboo Against Knowing Who You Are* (New York: Random House, 1966, 1989).

———. *The Spirit of Zen* (London: Murray, 1955).

Henry Wei, *The Guiding Light of Lao Tzu: A New Translation of the "Tao Te Ching"* (Wheaton, IL: Theosophical Publishing House, 1988).

CHAPTER 3: ACCEPTING THE TRUTH—BUDDHA

Gunarantana Bhante, *Mindfulness in Plain English* (Boston: Wisdom Publications, 1993).

Lama Surya Das, *Awakening the Buddha Within: Tibetan Wisdom for the Western World* (New York: Broadway Books/Bantam Doubleday, 1997).

Joseph Goldstein, *Insight Meditation: The Practice of Freedom* (Boston: Shambhala, 1994).

Jon Kabat-Zinn, *Wherever You Go, There You Are: Mindfulness Meditation in Everyday Life* (New York: Hyperion, 1994).

Jack Kornfield, *A Path with Heart* (New York: Bantam, 1993).

Stephen Levine, *A Gradual Awakening* (New York: Doubleday, 1979).

Thich Nhat Hanh, *Present Moment, Wonderful Moment* (Berkeley, CA: Parallax, 1990).

———. *Breathe: You Are Alive: Commentaries on "The Sutra on the Full Awareness of Breathing"* (Berkeley, CA: Parallax Press, 1988).

Nyamgal Rinpoche, *The Breath of Awakening* (Kinmet, Ontario: Bodhi, 1992).

Sharon Salzberg, *A Heart as Wide as the World: The Path of Lovingkindness* (Boston: Shambhala, 1999).

Nanamoli Thera, *Mindfulness of Breathing* (Sri Lanka: Buddhist Publication Society, 1982).

Chogyam Trungpa, *Shambhala: The Sacred Path of the Warrior* (Boston: Shambhala, 1984).

John Welwood, *Awakening the Heart* (Boston: Shambhala, 1983).

CHAPTER 4: HEART AWAKENING—JESUS

Jacques Beevers, *The Autobiography of St. Therese of Lisieux* (New York: Doubleday, 1971).

Christopher Bryant, *Jung and the Christian Way* (London: Darton, 1983).

Andrew Harvey, *Son of Man: The Mystical Path to Christ* (New York: Jeremy Tarcher/Putnam, 1998).

W. R. Inge, *Christian Mysticism* (New York: Meridian Books, 1956).

William James, *The Varieties of Religious Experience* (New York: University Books, 1963).

Byron Katie, *Loving What Is* (New York: Random House, 2002).

C. S. Lewis, *Mere Christianity* (New York: Macmillan, 1943).

D. C. Matt, *The Essential Kabbalah* (San Francisco: HarperSanFrancisco, 1997).

Thomas Merton, *Contemplative Prayer* (New York: Doubleday, 1969).

Stephen Mitchell, ed., *The Enlightened Mind: An Anthology of Sacred Prose* (New York: HarperCollins, 1991).

Joan Oliver, *Contemplative Living* (New York: Omega/Dell, 2000).

Evelyn Underhill, *The Mystics of the Church* (New York: Schocken, 1964).

CHAPTER 5: EMOTIONAL HEALING—MOHAMMED

Tor Andrae, *Mohammed and His Faith* (Mineola, NY: Dover, 1955, 1999).

Thomas Cleary, trans., *The Essential Koran: The Heart of Islam* (San Francisco: HarperSanFrancisco, 1993).

David Cooper, *God Is a Verb* (New York: Riverhead Books, 1997).

Kabir Helminski, *The Knowing Heart: A Sufi Path of Transformation* (Boston: Shambhala, 1999).

Robert Nicholson, *The Mystics of Islam* (London: Routledge Press, 1963).

Neal Robinson, *Islam: A Concise Introduction* (Washington, DC: George Washington University Press, 1999).

CHAPTER 6: SELF-REMEMBERING—GURDJIEFF

Martin Buber, *Tales of the Hasidim* (New York: Schocken, 1947).

Sophie Burnham, *The Ecstatic Journey* (New York: Ballantine, 1997).

Carlos Castaneda, *Journey to Ixlan* (New York: Ballantine, 1972).

———. *A Separate Reality* (New York: Ballantine, 1972).

Vivianne Crowley, *Jungian Spirituality* (New York: HarperCollins, 1998).

Sigmund Freud, *The Future of an Illusion* (New York: W. W. Norton, 1927).

G. I. Gurdjieff, *Meetings with Remarkable Men* (New York: Penguin Arcana, 1963).

Carl Jung, *Memories, Dreams, Reflections* (New York: Fontana, 1995).

Peter Russell, *Waking up in Time* (Novato, CA: Origin Press, 1998).

Robert Segal, *The Gnostic Jung* (Princeton, NJ: Princeton University Press, 1993).

Rami Shapiro, *Wisdom of the Jewish Sages: Pirke Avot* (New York: Harmony Books, 1993).

Gary Snyder, *The Practice of the Wild* (New York: Farrrar, Straus & Giroux, 1990).

CHAPTER 7: EXPERIENCING BLISS—KRISHNAMURTI

David Bohm, *Wholeness and the Implicate Order* (Boston: Routledge and Kegan Paul, 1980).

Albert Einstein, *Out of My Later Years* (New York: Philosophical Library, 1950).

Marcel Eliade, *The Sacred and the Profane* (New York: Harcourt Brace, 1957).

Aldous Huxley, *The Perennial Philosophy* (New York: Meridian, 1970).

J. Krishnamurti, *The Brockwood Talks* (Berkeley, CA: Shambhala, 1970).

———. *The Awakening of Intelligence* (New York: Harper & Row, 1973).

J. Krishnamurti and David Bohm, *The Limits of Thought* (New York: Routledge Press, 1999).

Claudio Naranjo, *The Psychology of Meditation* (New York: Viking Press, 1971).

Carl Rogers, *On Becoming a Person* (Boston: Houghton Mifflin, 1961).

Bertrand Russell, *Mysticism and Logic* (New York: Anchor Books, 1957).

Radha Rajagopal Sloss, *Lives in the Shadow with J. Krishnamurti* (New York: Bloomsbury Press, 1991).

Paul Tillich, *Systematic Theology* (Chicago: University of Chicago Press, 1963).

Online Free-Access Code

If you reach an area on the website for *Seven Masters* book owners only, please enter the ISBN number found on the copyright page for immediate free access to advanced programs.